# Victoria,
## My Daughter

# List of Plates

*Between pages 48 and 49*

1. Victoria and Demelza visit Sefton before the big parade (*Daily Mail*)
2. At home, May 1983 (*Daily Express*)
3. Victoria riding her bicycle after the amputation. She won the medal she is wearing in the school gymnastics display (*Daily Express*)
4. Joanna and Victoria on their way to school

*Between pages 96 and 97*

5. Joanna pushing Victoria in the go-cart she helped to make
6. Who said I can't climb trees?

*Between pages 128 and 129*

7, 8, 9. On holiday in Spain, June 1983
10. A treasured memory always

# Foreword

Victoria has inspired many with her courage. She still continues to do so through the fund for cancer research founded in her memory, in the hope that one day no family will have to go through what we and many others like us have had to. I would also like to think that these words are a tribute, not only to Victoria, but to all children and their families whose courage is never acknowledged and who probably never hit the headlines, but who nevertheless face what they have to with bravery and dignity.

# CHAPTER
## 1

August 1982 was nearly over. Autumn would soon be here, bringing with it the usual damp and miserable weather. We had already had a fairly busy year. Victoria had celebrated her tenth birthday in July and, much to my relief, had not wanted a birthday party. Instead we had a day out, to visit a house of historical interest, taking her sister and best friend Emma with us.

My parents had travelled from Cumbria to stay with us for nearly three weeks. This was no mean feat in a small house, with only two bedrooms, which we were renting at the time. We were in the process of building a new house, and had been lucky to find any house to rent, at least in the price bracket we could afford. This would be our seventh move in only twelve years of marriage, ranging from a tiny two up and two down cottage to what would now be a detached four-bedroomed house with a large garden. I was determined this would be the last.

Glancing at the clock on that Sunday morning of the August Bank Holiday weekend, I vaguely wondered where the time had gone: surely it could not possibly be ten o'clock already? Joanna, who had turned seven the previous April, was not even dressed yet. I had better tell the girls to hurry up.

'Oh, we're not going over to the new house again are we?' asked Victoria, in a disappointed tone, as she entered the kitchen in time to see me putting sandwiches and a flask into the basket on the table. 'It's so boring, there's nothing for Joanna and me to do. Can't we go swimming instead? Please, you did say we could soon.'

I could understand that they did get a little fed up: it was not much fun for them, seeing our future home taking shape. It did not seem to worry them that we wanted to finish the house as quickly as possible, as the smallness of this one was beginning to drive me mad. We had too much furniture for its size and it always seemed to be in a state of utter chaos.

'Well, I really meant that we might be able to go swimming later on,' I tried to explain. 'We'll have to take the food over anyway, as Daddy hasn't taken anything with him, but I suppose we needn't stay that long. Perhaps we could go swimming later on, all right?' It was the weekend after all.

'I suppose so,' she answered grudgingly. 'But Joanna and I are staying in the car to play.'

I did not argue with this. They had stayed in the car on a previous weekend visit and had not come to any harm, playing with their dolls and imagining that they were on some really exciting journey. Besides, I thought, it does tend to be rather cold in a newly-built house even in the summer, unless one is busy painting or shifting materials.

'Do you think you could ask Joanna to hurry up please? She's still in her nightdress. We won't be there in time for tea at this rate, never mind lunch. I'll just tidy up in here and then we'll go.'

She went off to sort Joanna out, which was not going to be easy, if the screams and giggles reaching me from the sitting room were anything to go by. Still, they had to let off steam sometimes.

I started to wash the few dishes in the sink, thinking that at least it was not too long now until the end of September, when we hoped the new house would be ready. We had been working hard at weekends, particularly Alan, my husband, who had been there every single day since we had started the building. That was mainly why we went over too, otherwise we would hardly have seen anything of him. At least now the house had reached a stage where I could help out with some of the painting and tidying up.

Looking out of the kitchen window, I noticed our family doctor on the other side of the green. We had not had much contact with him during our temporary residence here. I wondered vaguely which house he was looking for, as he checked the numbers of those opposite. I turned away to get a tea towel from the hook behind me, and as I turned back I was surprised that he was now walking towards our house. Whatever for, I wondered? I had not called him out. He was probably just coming to ask directions. Then a terrible thought occurred to me. Was he coming about Victoria's knee? No, don't be ridiculous I thought, it couldn't possibly be about that. She had only had the X-ray taken on Friday, just the day before yesterday. He couldn't know anything already. Anyway, it surely wasn't serious? Victoria had only mentioned the fact that it was painful about ten days ago. It had become worse though, even in the last couple of days. No, I was being thoroughly stupid, she had just twisted it or something, which was the reason I had taken her to the doctor in the first place. As she said she hadn't knocked it, I had been rather surprised that she was even sent for an X-ray.

The sound of the door bell dismissed these thoughts from my mind. I was being neurotic about it anyway, so I opened the door ready to direct the doctor to the right house, convincing myself this was the reason for his visit. I was slightly taken aback when, after apologising for calling on a Sunday, he asked if he might come in.

'No, of course, that's all right,' I stammered, my fears returning as he asked if there was somewhere we might talk privately. The girls, of course, had rushed into the hall when they heard him and were obviously eager to know what the doctor was doing there. They went upstairs, however, without too much trouble, ostensibly to tidy their bedroom, as I directed him through to the main room.

As we both sat down I glanced rather nervously behind me, to see that the door was shut properly. What was he going to say? Why was he here? He looked nervous and ill at ease, the more so when he discovered that Alan was not in and I was on my own.

'I'm sorry to have to tell you that I have come about Victoria's knee.'

Oh my God, I had been right, there was something wrong.

'I'm afraid the X-ray has shown the formation of a tumour on the bone. The Radiographer noticed it and got in touch with me. I've already been in touch with the Consultant Orthopaedic Surgeon at the hospital and he too has seen the X-rays. He's made a study of this type of bone cancer, so Victoria will be in good hands.'

Tumour? Bone cancer? Oh God, it could not be true,

not cancer? Not Victoria! Why could it not have been me?

Fighting back my tears, still unable to comprehend what he had said, I asked if there was a chance that they might be wrong about it. Surely they couldn't be so certain at this stage? My heart sank as he said they were fairly certain and were experienced at interpreting the X-rays. He went on to say that the Consultant would like to see us with Victoria tomorrow. But it was Bank Holiday Monday.

It must be true then. They do not see routine cases at such times. I couldn't believe it, couldn't take it in. Why? Why? I was quite calm outwardly now, but my mind was in a turmoil. This could not be happening, not to us: this only happened to other people one read about in women's magazines or saw programmes about on television. I felt hurt and angry, betrayed in some way. I wished desperately that Alan was here with me, that I didn't feel so alone. The doctor seemed to guess how I felt. He asked if I could get in touch with Alan at the house. When I told him that there was no telephone as yet, he suggested that I should take the girls over as soon as possible and not stay on my own.

'I know this must have come as a terrible shock to you, but is there anything you would like to ask me before I leave?'

There were a hundred things I wanted to know, but I couldn't sort out the jumble of thoughts flashing through my mind. Sensing how confused I was he said, 'Treatment for cancer has advanced greatly during the last few years and, although I am no expert, it can be cured if it is caught early enough.' I didn't ask if we were early enough, terrified of what he might say.

Having made sure we knew where the hospital was and where we had to go when we arrived, he rose to leave. 'I can't tell you how sorry I am to be the bearer of such bad news,' he said. 'It is one of the worst aspects of this job, one that nevertheless has to be done, but one never gets used to it. Well, goodbye, I'll be in touch and if you ever want to see me about anything, don't hesitate to phone me at any time.'

Thanking him for his kindness, I closed the door behind him, almost with relief, my head still spinning. I couldn't think straight, couldn't imagine what to do first. Hearing the girls on their way down the stairs, I realised I would have to pull myself together quickly. They must not know that there was anything wrong. I had hardly had time to conjure up some explanation for the doctor's visit, when the inevitable question came from Victoria.

'Why was the doctor here? Aren't you well?'

'Oh, I'm fine,' I prevaricated. What could I say? I certainly couldn't tell them the real reason for his visit. They would of course have to know about tomorrow's visit to the hospital but I wanted to talk to Alan first, to decide on the best way to explain it. 'He just happened to be in the area and called in to say that the results of a test I had done a few weeks ago were fine. He thought I might like to know.'

It didn't sound very convincing to me but at least there was some truth in it, I had had a test done. They seemed quite content with my answer anyway, and that was all that really mattered.

'If you're both ready, you can go round and get in the car. I'll just get the basket and lock the door. Daddy will wonder what on earth we've been doing all morning.'

They scampered off without a care in the world, blissfully unaware that there was anything wrong, thank goodness. With a heavy heart I locked the door and followed them, wondering for the umpteenth time why, oh why did it have to be Victoria?

It seemed to take forever to get to the new house, although it was only a journey of some eight miles. I was shaking so much when we did arrive that I wondered how I had managed to drive there at all. I certainly hadn't been concentrating, thinking all the time about what the doctor had said and what I was going to say to Alan. How on earth could I tell him anything with the girls there? With enormous relief, I remembered Victoria having said earlier that they wanted to play in the car. I prayed that they wouldn't change their minds. For that reason I didn't even ask them if they were coming into the house. I simply gave them a packet of crisps each and almost ran up to the front door, at the same time trying to behave normally. Alan must have heard the car for he was standing just inside, having opened the door for me. I rushed inside and threw myself into his comforting arms, finally allowing myself the luxury of breaking down, which, looking back on it, must have been hard for him as he didn't know what was going on.

'What on earth's wrong?' he asked, completely bewildered. 'Have you had an accident?'

'No, it's Victoria,' I managed to blurt out. 'The doctor has just been round, about that X-ray she had, remember, last Friday? They think it's a tumour on the bone. We've got to take her to see a specialist tomorrow. As soon as I saw the doctor there, I had this terrible feeling there was something wrong. I never imagined anything like this.'

'They must be able to remove it, surely. What did he say?'

I stared at him in disbelief. How could he be so calm and matter-of-fact about something like this? Then I realised with horror that I had omitted to tell him the worst aspect of all.

'Oh Alan,' I sobbed, 'they think it's cancer. She's got cancer.'

He was visibly shaken, but even after what I had just said he seemed so much more calm than me. I felt sure that either he had not taken in fully what I had said, or worse still, he thought I had misunderstood what I had been told.

'Come and sit in here and have some coffee,' he said, guiding me through to what would eventually become our sitting room, where the only furniture so far was our garden chairs. He asked me exactly what the doctor had said, and as he poured out the coffee I told him all that I remembered, trying hard not to forget anything. We now had to decide what we were going to tell Victoria, so that we would both say the same thing. We decided for now just to tell her that something very small had been found to be wrong with her knee and that we would all find out more about it after tomorrow's visit to the hospital. We hoped Victoria would find nothing unusual in the fact that it was a public holiday. We would just have to hope that she would not ask too many questions that we would be unable to answer. We would have to play it very much by ear. We certainly could not make any plans for what she might ask. We had no idea.

'What about our parents? We'll have to tell them something, won't we?' asked Alan. 'On the other hand, it does seem a bit silly to worry them just yet, at least until we know a bit more ourselves.'

'I think we should let them know something, at least warn them,' I said, feeling that it might bring us a sense of comfort to share the terrible news with our immediate family. Then we began to wonder how we could even talk about it with the girls around, never mind start phoning relatives.

'I did half promise to take them swimming later on, although I must admit I don't feel much like it now; but at least if I did that, you would be able to use the phone while they are out of the house.'

Having decided that this was the best course of action, Alan began cleaning the paint brushes he had been using when I had arrived. 'We'll get going then, shall we?' he said.

'Won't the girls think it a bit odd if we leave now? We've only just got here.'

We looked helplessly at one another, neither of us knowing quite what to do for the best. It was Alan who spoke first, voicing my own thoughts as he said, 'Well, perhaps we should just finish painting the walls in the kitchen. I don't think I could sit around doing nothing anyway. Perhaps after you've taken them for a swim we could go out for a drive or something? Anything rather than sit about at home.'

I stood up to follow him through to the hall. Halfway there he stopped and turned to face me. Putting his arms round me he said, 'One thing is for sure, I don't care if we have to sell this house and everything else we own, Victoria will have the best treatment there is, even if we have to go abroad to find it.'

We had almost finished the painting when the front door burst open and the girls rushed in. 'Can't we go now? We're fed up with playing in the car,' said Joanna. 'Yes, and you did say we could go swimming,' added Victoria.

Alan and I looked briefly at each other, questioning the advisability of suddenly downing tools and agreeing to their demands. In normal circumstances, they would just have to wait until we were ready, but nothing felt normal any more.

It was Alan who answered them. 'Just let us finish this one wall. It's the last one in here and then at least one room will be finished. Then you can go swimming while I have a bath and get changed, then perhaps we can all go out somewhere together?'

'Ooh, yes please,' came the chorus in reply.

'Well, there are some sandwiches left in the other room if you're hungry, and some orange squash,' I said. 'We won't be very long now.'

They scampered off happily, soon arguing over the last packet of crisps. We completed our tasks, each of us wishing and hoping that tomorrow's visit would not turn out to be as bad as we feared.

The rest of the day will always remain a blurred and hazy memory. It passed with a sense of unreality, like being in a trance. Sleepwalking. Or as if we were watching a play or film about other people, yet, at the same time knowing that the players were ourselves. All I could think of was, why Victoria? Why did it have to happen to her? It was so unfair. I went through every emotion, from despair to anger and resentment, aimed at whom I didn't know. All the time feeling so helpless. We had no answers as yet to all the things we wanted to know.

As I watched them splashing about in the pool,

laughing and happy with all the carefree joy that only children seem able to display, it was impossible to believe that any of what I had been told that fateful morning was true, that she might have cancer. How could anyone who looked as well as she did possibly have that dreaded and feared disease? Then I recalled having read somewhere that it often doesn't affect the sufferer's outward physical appearance. I remembered too that the pain in her knee had worsened even in the last few days. Why hadn't I worried about it sooner? Taken her to the doctor as soon as she had first mentioned it? But I had never imagined that it would turn out to be anything so serious. Children are always knocking themselves and complaining of little aches and pains. I had really thought I was making a fuss over nothing by taking her to the doctor in the first place. If only I could have known. Should I have taken more notice sooner? Would I ever rid myself of this terrible feeling of guilt?

Arriving home from the pool, I had no way of knowing whether Alan had managed any of the telephone calls to relatives that we had discussed earlier. I couldn't ask him in front of Victoria and Joanna, they would immediately start to wonder why. However, he must have realised how anxious I was; as I returned from hanging the wet towels and costumes in the garden, he said, quite casually, 'Oh, by the way, Sheila phoned while you were out, I told her you would either phone her back later tonight or sometime tomorrow.'

'I'll leave it until tomorrow. We might be late back if we're going out now.' The fact was that I felt sure I would have even more need of my sister's comfort after tomorrow's appointment. I also realised that Alan would have told her as much as we already knew.

Although I didn't know exactly what Alan had told anyone during the course of the calls, at least I knew now that he had managed to make them. He would tell me later, when the girls were in bed and asleep. It was going to be no easy task, constantly checking ourselves in case we let something slip. Whatever else happened, the last thing we wanted was for either of them to be worried or frightened in any way. The thought that they might overhear half of a conversation, misinterpret the meaning and then worry about it without telling either Alan or myself, was always on our minds.

So it was with some relief that we came downstairs later that evening, after seeing the girls safely in bed. They were exhausted, and so were we, as it had been quite late when we had returned from our drive to the coast. That and their earlier swim sent them straight to sleep.

Alan and I talked late into the night, as we were to do on many more nights to come, checking every half-hour or so, that the girls were indeed asleep. That night we spoke mainly of what Alan had said over the phone to my sister and Victoria's grandparents. Apart from the impending visit to the hospital the following day and the fact that cancer was suspected, we knew so little. And knowing so little, it was difficult to talk about it without covering the same ground over and over again.

We both felt that it would be best to wait and see what we would find out, still hoping that it would prove to be some kind of terrible mistake. At the same time we both realised that mistakes such as that are rarely made.

As to our parents, Alan's were staying in Devon with his sister and her family. They had only motored down on the previous Friday, but of course wanted to come straight back on hearing the news. He had tried to dissuade them but to no avail. They were already on their way. Although there was nothing they could do I think they just wanted to be with us. Indeed, their support over the next few days proved invaluable.

My parents, however, were a different matter. Apart from being a little older than Alan's, it was the effect that the news might have on my mother in particular that worried us. She had suffered from depression in the past and still took drugs to keep it at bay. The last thing we wanted was for our news to cause a recurrence of these problems. Consequently Alan and Sheila had decided between them that it might be best to tell them nothing at this stage, at least not until we knew a little more ourselves.

Sleep was almost impossible. Most of the night, once we had finally retired upstairs, was spent tossing and turning, going over all that we knew so far and still hoping against hope that it would turn out that someone had got it wrong. Realistically, we both knew that the most we could hope for now was that the cancer had been discovered in time and could be treated. Anything else just didn't bear thinking about. One seldom hears of a child with cancer, although there had been a lot of publicity fairly recently about bone marrow transplants to cure leukaemia. Yet we have since found out that cancer is the second biggest killer of children after accidents, including accidents in the home. A sobering thought indeed: but of course one always expects it to happen to someone else, never to one's own beloved child.

# CHAPTER
## 2

August Bank Holiday Monday, 1982, dawned dull and overcast. It seemed that even the weather had conspired against us. Our appointment with the Consultant was to take place in the early afternoon, which left hours to pass until it was time to leave for his office at the hospital. Hours that seemed to pass with agonising slowness. Half the time wishing that they would pass quickly, so that it would all be over, yet at the same time hoping the hour of reckoning would never come, not wanting to know the truth of what the doctor had told me the previous day.

I glanced at the clock yet again, only to discover that just a few minutes had passed since I had last looked. Eventually, however, it was time to leave. Victoria, not surprisingly, was a little apprehensive by this time. We had told her the day before when we were in the car that something very small, possibly a tiny crack in the bone, had been seen in the X-ray. Her first question, of course, had been to ask why I had not told her that this had been the true reason for the doctor's visit yesterday. 'I wouldn't have been upset, you know.'

I apologised for telling a white lie and explained that I had wanted to talk to Alan about it first, so that we could tell her together. She seemed to accept this explanation philosophically. She said she wasn't worried about it, but she must have been a little anxious and we felt she was bottling it up, not wanting us to worry on her behalf.

The only one to seem completely unconcerned about the whole thing was Joanna, who kept up an incessant flow of chatter throughout the journey to the hospital. That relieved the tension slightly, although most of it fell on deaf ears and I found it hard to restrain myself from telling her to be quiet.

The various clinics were not open because of the holiday. We had been told to report to the Accident and Emergency Centre at the hospital, and we would be shown the way to the Fracture Clinic. As we entered through the plate glass doors, Alan and I looked at one another over the girls' heads, a reassurance that no matter what, we would always be together in everything. We didn't have to face anything alone. We had had our ups and downs, what married couple has not, but these past differences had only served to strengthen our relationship.

After we had given our names to the sister at the reception desk we sat down to wait, sensing that the staff knew exactly why we were there. It was not long before a door opened and a gentleman in a dark suit emerged and walked towards us. He introduced himself as Mr Steel, the Consultant Orthopaedic Surgeon who was to see Victoria. His manner and way of speaking put us at ease as much as was possible under the circumstances. He asked us to follow him through to the clinic, where he also had his office, but he told Victoria he would have a look at her knee in the clinic first.

The out-patients' clinic turned out to be fairly large

and typical. The usual curtained off examination couches ranged down either side of the walls. We followed Mr Steel into one of these where he asked Victoria if she could manage to get onto the couch on her own. 'Of course I can,' she replied and then demonstrated. He asked her one or two questions as he performed his examination, such as how bad the pain was and whether it had become worse recently.

'Oh it's not bad really,' she answered, almost in a whisper. She tended to be rather shy with people she did not know well. 'But I couldn't get to sleep last night and Mummy gave me a pillow to put under it.'

'Did that help a little?'

She nodded silently in reply, and we could all see her trying not to wince as he manipulated her knee. Having finished his examination, he asked the girls if they would mind waiting where they were so that he could have a word with Alan and me in his office. He explained that what he had to say wouldn't be very interesting for them.

'I know what little girls are like,' he said jovially. 'Can't sit still for five minutes. There are some toys in here that you can play with while you're waiting.' They had already spotted the toys and seemed quite content to stay where they were.

'We won't be long,' I said, as we followed Mr Steel through into his office. 'See you in a minute.'

Once inside the office we sat down, hardly daring to draw breath as he opened the file in front of him. 'I'm sorry to call you in like this. It must have been a shock for you. Your own doctor did see you yesterday, didn't he?'

We both nodded, unable to speak. Eventually I managed to say, 'He said there is a tumour on the bone and that it might be cancer?' hoping that he would immediately refute this and say that some mistake had been made.

That tenuous hope was soon dashed by his next words as he said, 'Well, I'm afraid it's virtually certain even at this stage, although of course I will perform a biopsy to confirm my diagnosis. I've had fairly extensive experience of this type of cancer and I'm afraid there really is no doubt in my mind.'

He paused for a moment, to let us digest what he had said thus far before continuing, 'I think it will be best if I explain exactly what it is and how it has to be dealt with. Then you can ask any questions you might have.' Again we nodded in silent unison, at the same time taking hold of each other's hands, as if by doing so we were gaining strength from each other in some way.

'The biopsy will, I'm sure, confirm the fact that it is a rare type of cancer called Osteogenic Sarcoma. It is a very virulent form of cancer, especially in a child. Unless it is stopped, its spread is extremely rapid.' He cleared his throat, somewhat nervously I felt. 'I'm afraid it means that her leg will have to be amputated.'

Oh my God! No, he couldn't mean it. I felt as if I had been struck physically: one look at Alan's face was enough to tell me that he felt the same.

'If it is allowed to spread, it will eventually find its way into her lungs. I don't think I need to tell you how serious that would be. She will, as a matter of course, be given radiotherapy treatment anyway, in case one or two stray cells have already broken away from the original tumour.'

To say that we were stunned, devastated or any other similar adjective, would be an understatement. Even in our wildest nightmares we could never have imagined that it would be as bad as this. It was too awful even to contemplate how Victoria would take it when she found out the truth. Had I quite understood what he had said? I must surely have misunderstood him. I looked at Alan, and realised that I had misunderstood nothing. How could we possibly tell Victoria? How could anyone? I think I would have sold my soul to the devil at that moment if it would have changed things. If only it could have been me instead.

As if he knew what we were both thinking Mr Steel said, 'At this stage I will just tell Victoria that there is a small crack on her knee and that I want to operate to have a better look at it. We will have to take it one step at a time, as far as she is concerned, but I have found in cases like this that it is the parents who have more difficulty in accepting something, which is after all a mutilation in their eyes, than the child. The important thing is to gain her confidence and trust and thereby not to tell her any outright lies, but instead to try and answer her questions as truthfully as possible, but without the full implication of exactly what it is, so as not to frighten her in any way.'

I felt he was so right in all of what he had just said. As a mother I had already discovered that children only want to know so much at any one time and therefore it is best to tell the truth. Yet still I could not believe that this nightmare was really happening. Why did it have to be us? Worst of all why did it have to be Victoria? It all seemed so unfair.

I heard Alan asking Mr Steel if this was our only hope. Was there no alternative? 'What about chemotherapy?'

'I'm afraid there really is no other option available to us. Her case has already been discussed with the Consultant Radiologist in charge of cancer treatment; it was decided that chemotherapy at this stage, after the trauma of the amputation, would be too much for one so young. That is why radiotherapy will be used afterwards.'

'What about her chances after the amputation?' Alan asked.

'I'm afraid I can't put them any higher than about twenty per cent, even then. The first two or three years are the most critical, but we could not say with any certainty until five years have passed without the cancer recurring. She will have three-monthly checkups for that reason. Her chances will obviously increase the longer she goes without any recurrence.'

So, even after the amputation our worries would not be over. We would constantly be waiting to see if there were any signs of a return. It would be like living on a knife edge.

Mr Steel went on to explain that while Victoria was in hospital for the biopsy, she would also undergo various bone and body scans amongst other tests, to make sure that the cancer had not already spread, which left us with yet another new and even more terrifying thought. It had never occurred to me that it might have spread somewhere else. Please God it had not.

He told us that the piece of bone removed for analysis would be fairly small and should cause her the minimum of discomfort. It would take about a week for the results to come through, and then Victoria would have to be told. How? Who was going to tell her? I just couldn't imagine having to impart such a terrible, and surely to a child, terrifying news. Again he seemed to sense how we were both feeling as he said, 'Would you like me to tell her? It might be easier if it came from me, unless you feel you would like to do it. Of course you would be with her at the time.'

We both thanked him and said we would like him to tell her, although what would happen when he did could only be imagined and filled me with dread. The last ten minutes or so had completely turned our world upside down. Again I wondered, would things ever be the same again?

Mr Steel felt that we ought to be getting back to the girls or they would begin to wonder what was going on. I glanced at Alan, only then realising with a shock how devastated he was. I had never seen him cry before and my heart went out to him. It is strange looking back that we rarely broke down at the same time, as if we each of us knew that we had to comfort the other. My turn would come later. He had to pull himself together before we went back into the clinic, but he was marvellous and no-one would have ever guessed there was anything wrong.

The girls were brought to a standstill by our appearance. They had obviously been charging about in the empty room, the novelty of the toys having long since worn off.

'Well, Victoria,' said Mr Steel, as he walked over to her, 'I've just been telling Mummy and Daddy that it looks as if there might be a small crack on your knee and I would like to have a closer look at it. So I would like you to come into the children's ward here tomorrow and have a very small operation. You won't mind that, will you?'

'Tomorrow? Gosh, that's quick. How long will I have to stay?' she asked, apprehensively, beginning to bite at her bottom lip, always a sign of nerves.

'Not long, just for a couple of days. You'll be home for

the weekend. That won't be too bad, will it?'

'No, I suppose not. Is it just for an operation?'

'Well, there are one or two tests I would like you to have done, as you will be here anyway: but certainly nothing painful, nothing to worry about, and you'll like the children's ward. They have a playroom and television, of course.'

Victoria seemed quite happy about all this. We followed to the office where a form was typed for her admission the next day. This was where he left us, saying to Victoria that he would see her in the morning. He was so kind. I was so glad that if this had to happen, at least he would help us through as much as possible. He seemed already to have a certain rapport with Victoria, whose feelings were after all paramount.

I tucked the form safely away in my handbag and we made our way out to the car park, Victoria skipping along by my side holding my hand.

'You're not too worried about it, are you?' I asked anxiously.

'I was worried for a bit. I thought he was going to tell me I had to have my leg cut off.'

I was completely dumbfounded. Lord, was there never going to be an end to these shocks? What on earth would she say when she found out the truth of what she had just said: she had sounded so relieved. Thankfully she chattered on about tomorrow's visit. I couldn't speak.

Once we were in the car and on our way, Victoria wanted to know all about operations and anaesthetics and what it was like to be in hospital? Would the nurses be nice? We could sense that she was quite looking forward to it in a way. It would be a new adventure, something to tell her friends at school when she went back. Alan and I looked at each other. She would not be going back to school for some time—another thing she was yet to discover.

We had decided to go to Alan's parents' home on our return. We didn't feel we could cope on our own at home for the moment. I noticed we had driven past their gate.

'Where are we going?' I asked.

'I thought we would go to the new house,' Alan answered, 'Dad's working there. You can take the car up to Mum's. I'll come on later with Dad.'

It seemed a sensible idea. We would not be able to say anything to either of his parents in front of the girls anyway, and at least this way he would be able to tell his father who could warn his mother later.

I realised, however, that this was not the only reason for the detour. Alan was having a hard time controlling his emotions and he didn't want the girls to see how upset he was and perhaps to start asking questions.

'Let me drive?' I said, feeling utterly helpless.

'No, it's all right. Have you got some tissues?' I handed him one as Victoria, ever observant, said 'What's wrong with Daddy? Is he crying?'

'No, no of course not, he's just got hay fever.' Could one get hay fever in late August? But what else could I say? I just hoped that she would not think it slightly strange that he had never suffered from it before.

He was out of the car and away as soon as he had stopped. Glancing in the mirror I could see his father coming out to meet him. I drove off quickly, so that no-one else could see the expression on Alan's father's face as he saw his son. He knew in that instant that something dreadful had happened.

Arriving at their house, the girls were out of the car

almost before I had turned the ignition off and, when I reached the door, Victoria had already divulged her exciting news to a rather bewildered granny. As the girls went into the sitting room to see if there was anything interesting on the 'box', Mum said, 'It's not as bad as you thought then?'

'It's worse,' was all I could say. 'But I can't say anything now. Victoria doesn't know anything. Dad will be able to tell you everything later. Alan is with him now.'

She made me a cup of coffee and chatted away about this and that, but I don't remember a single thing she said. I just couldn't keep my mind on anything, although I suppose I must have answered her. But at least it kept me from breaking down completely. I wondered how Alan was and how his father was taking it all. I thought yet again how difficult it was going to be, trying to pretend that everything was normal, but we had to make sure that the girls knew nothing, least of all how upset and worried we were. That would have frightened them. Then, too, there was Joanna. How was she going to take it? We had been so worried on Victoria's behalf that we had hardly spared her younger sister a second thought. Not that we had had much time to think about anything yet. It really had not sunk in fully. It still felt as if it was a dream. Oh, if only that could have been the case.

There was also the question of school which I had thought about briefly in the car. Would she still be able to go to the convent, where they were both so happy? I so hoped she would. Although we are not Catholics, we found the school to be very good for our two and they had many friends there. Religion was never forced on anyone.

There were many things, as yet unknown, that would have to be discussed. But we realised that day that it was perhaps best not to look too far ahead, but to take each day as it came. That is, after all, how children cope with life. They only think about today and tomorrow and are not too concerned about next month or next year. I have often thought they could teach us adults a thing or two. After all, none of us knows what life has in store for us.

At last Alan and his father arrived, both of them looking ghastly, the pain etched into their faces for all to see. The girls, naturally, rushed through to the kitchen to see Grandad. My heart missed a beat. They were bound to notice that something was wrong. But no, both Dad and Alan managed to pull themselves together and put on a bright smile.

Dad had suggested going out for a drive and perhaps having a meal somewhere. None of us felt we could sit around staring at one another, trying to make bright conversation. It was only after he had left the room to go and get changed, that Victoria called me aside, 'I want to say something to you in private Mummy,' she said. Taking me into a corner she asked me if Grandad had been crying. This really brought home to me how absolutely vital it was going to be for us all to act normally. I swiftly managed to reply, 'Whatever makes you think that? I think he's just got a cold.'

'Well, it seems funny that Daddy's suddenly got hay fever and now Grandad's got a cold. I don't want anybody to cry about me. I'm going to be all right you know, Mummy. Tell them not to worry.'

I was amazed. Had we really been so unsuccessful in our subterfuge? But no, I didn't think it was that as much as the fact that Victoria just didn't want to feel we were worrying on her behalf. She was certainly not at all worried. But I had a quiet word with everyone. I didn't want the situation to get any worse.

During the rest of the day it was the girls themselves who kept us going. With their bright chatter and laughter, they certainly made things much easier for us all. But I for one found it very hard at times to keep back the tears, thinking over and over again of what the Consultant had told us earlier. It demanded a supreme effort to try and keep up the artificial brightness that none of us felt.

It was again with a certain sense of relief that later on that night, after the girls were safely tucked up in bed, Alan and I could talk freely. It had all happened so fast. Only yesterday we had been told of the likelihood that Victoria had cancer. Now, just twenty-four hours later, we knew that she was to go into hospital the following morning for a biopsy which would confirm the almost certain fact that her left leg would have to be amputated.

How well would we all, and especially Victoria herself, cope with this? That was something we could not, as yet, know. Only time would tell.

# CHAPTER
## 3

The morning of Victoria's admission to hospital meant a fairly early start for us all, and if she wanted any breakfast it had to be eaten before eight o'clock. The operation was scheduled for the early part of the afternoon.

Seeing Victoria coming down the stairs with Joanna, both of them dressed, I was amazed to hear her announce that she was not hungry and, although I tried to persuade her at least to have some toast, she refused. That was as much to do with nerves as anything else, I felt.

The next big decision came as we were about to leave, when she said, 'Which toy shall I take with me?'

'Whichever one you like,' I replied, thinking that this might take all day. They had so many cuddly toys that choosing just one might not prove an easy task. One, however, was picked with surprising speed. Of course it was the oldest and dirtiest of all of them, and one she rarely played with at any other time, but no amount of persuasion would change her mind. The expression on Alan's face said it all. As we got into the car I found myself wishing that I had washed it.

Once at the hospital we made our way up to the children's ward in the lift. Victoria suddenly tugged at my hand. She wanted to tell me something, she said. I bent closer to hear what it was. I was stunned when she reiterated what she had told me the previous day. 'You and Daddy mustn't worry about me. I know you have been, but I'll be all right, you know.' I cannot explain exactly how I felt on hearing these words for the second time in as many days: I found myself wondering if she perhaps sensed in some way how serious things were?

These thoughts, however, fled from my mind as we entered the ward itself. It certainly was not like most hospitals I had been in before, with their long impersonal wards, lined on either side by rows of beds. Of course the hospital had been built only a few years previously and still had a new feel about it. Each ward consisted of small units of eight, six and two beds to a room. The friendly atmosphere as we walked in was almost palpable. We were so busy looking round us and taking it all in that we failed to notice the approach of two nurses.

'Hello, I'm Sister Ford and you must be Victoria. You can call me Sarah.' She introduced the other girl as Staff Nurse Mary, saying that she would be looking after her for today and preparing her for the operation. 'Would you like to choose which bed you are going to have? We haven't many children in today so you can have whichever one you like in here.' She showed us into the room in front of which we had been standing, which was close to the nurses' station, at the entrance to the ward.

The time before the operation passed fairly quickly, being taken up with various checks and a blood sample. This did not have much appeal for Victoria, but she underwent the ordeal with silent resignation.

Her face brightened when a young doctor, who introduced himself as Mr Steel's houseman, came to check

35

over her details. She took to him straight away. He also mentioned some of the tests to her. These I think had been worrying her, as we ourselves knew so little about them. Her fears were allayed by the way that both he and Sister explained things to her, and told her that Alan and I could always be with her, if she wanted us to be. We both came to admire the patient and kindly way that Sister and her staff dealt with their young charges. They were marvellous and always spoke to them in words they were able to understand, without ever patronising them in any way.

The operation was soon over. In fact Victoria was back on the ward within the hour and for the rest of the day drifted in and out of sleep, although she became fully awake at any attempt on our part to leave. We eventually managed to go, however, having promised to be back early the next day. We had all, Victoria included, decided that there was no need for either of us to stay at the hospital with her, as she was only going to be in for such a short time. She might change her mind on her next visit, as yet unknown to her.

It had been fairly late when we had eventually left her the previous evening. Consequently our arrival in the morning was not as early as we had intended. Victoria's accusing glance met us as we entered the room. 'You said you would be here early and it's after half-past nine,' she said close to tears.

'Oh darling, I'm sorry,' I replied, feeling so terribly guilty and selfish into the bargain. 'We did mean to be a little earlier, but even so, it's not that late, is it?'

'I thought you would be here about eight o'clock. I'd been awake for ages. Then they opened the curtains so early and I kept thinking that any minute you would be here.' Her bottom lip trembled slightly on these words. We put our arms around her, Joanna too, and gave her a cuddle, as if we could somehow make up for upsetting her.

'We'll try and be a little earlier tomorrow,' Alan promised, 'but we don't have any nurses to wake us up.'

'I'm sorry I'm being so mean,' said Victoria. 'It was just that I was worried they might take me for one of the tests before you got here and I didn't want to be on my own.'

'Well, we're here now, and I'm sure they wouldn't have done anything without us,' I said, by now feeling worse than ever about the whole thing. 'Did you manage to sleep all right?'

She proceeded to regale us with all the details of the previous night, and about the different nurses who were on duty. 'They sit out there and have their coffee and chatter all the time, I couldn't get to sleep,' she said. 'Then they kept waking me up to take my temperature.'

'I thought you just said that you couldn't sleep because they were chatting,' Joanna said accusingly. 'How come they had to wake you up if you couldn't go to sleep in the first place?' We all laughed and told her that she had probably slept much more than she imagined she had.

There were one or two staff nurses on duty who had not been there the day before. One of them, a tall, nice-looking girl, was tidying up the bed next to Victoria's. 'That's Jill, she's my friend,' we were all informed. 'Can I go to the playroom now Jill please?'

'I'll have to see about that,' Jill answered, with the vaguest hint of a north country accent. 'Have you had a wash and cleaned your teeth yet?'

'Yes.'

'Ooh, you fibber,' said Joanna. 'I never saw you.'

'That's because I did it before you got here, dumbo.' A

slight dig at us for being late. I did wish that they would not call each other these awful names, but I supposed that other parents had to put up with them too and it could have been something much worse.

Jill went off to see if she could find a wheelchair anywhere. She seemed very nice and I could see that Victoria had taken to her straight away. There seemed to be a certain rapport between them. Indeed, Jill was to become a special friend to us all in the months that followed; her husband too, who happened to be the curate at our local church.

A rather smart chair was found and Victoria was helped into it. 'Right, I'm off to do some painting. See you later Jill.' Off they went down the corridor, Joanna doing her best to push the chair, but after one or two near misses (during which time I imagine she was called a few more choice names), Alan took over.

'Isn't she going for the scan today?' I asked Jill, as we watched them disappear down the corridor.

'Yes, in about half an hour actually,' she answered, 'she won't have very long in the playroom, but I couldn't say no, she's talked of nothing else all morning. How about you, how are you coping?'

'Well, you know, just coping. I still can't believe any of this is really happening.'

'I know how you must be feeling,' she said thoughtfully. 'Well, I don't really know, no-one does, but I can imagine something of what you are going through. You all seem very close, which helps a lot.' She could not have said a truer word, being alone through all this would have been intolerable.

Victoria's painting trip that morning was a very brief one, and indeed the playroom saw little of her during this first visit to its environs. Now that the actual operation was over there were still all the tests to complete. She had already had the chest X-ray done the day before, prior to the operation, and we knew that it was clear. We were thankful that the disease had not already reached her lungs, which had been a possibility. We also knew that any individual cells would not show up on an ordinary X-ray. This was the reason for the course of radiotherapy later on.

The first of the scans to be done was the one using an I.C.T. whole Body Scanner. This would show any spread of the disease in the internal organs of the body and is achieved by the body passing very slowly through the machine, while X-ray type pictures are taken of cross sections of the body. These are then fed into a computer and the results can then be analysed by experts, thus allowing them to detect even very small areas of disease and allow early treatment.

Victoria had been a little apprehensive of having this scan, but once she had been assured that it would not hurt she was able to relax, and the only thing she had to contend with was the boredom. The scan took nearly two hours to complete and there was nothing she could do apart from lie on the table and stare at the ceiling. She even managed to fall asleep at times, according to Alan who had gone in with her. He had to wear an extremely heavy lead filled apron for protection against any potentially harmful rays.

The bone scan, too, took some hours to complete, due mainly to the fact that a coloured dye has to be injected, so that the bones show up on the scan. This process takes nearly two hours to allow penetration to occur fully, and it is this dye that shows the difference between healthy areas of bone and those touched by the disease. Again the results are all put on computer and analysed later. None of these results would be known to us immediately. More waiting and wondering. We were getting used to it by now.

My sister had motored down from her home in Cumbria, bringing with her our mother who had, by her strength and calmness about everything, proved our previous fears groundless. Alan had suggested the possibility that we ought to go away for the coming weekend, when Victoria came out this time and before the amputation took place. We certainly felt as if we could do with a break, but knew too that we could ill afford any extra expense at the present time. It would have been all too easy to spend money, as if to ease things and make up to Victoria in some way for what was going to happen. But we had to be sensible about it; no-one would benefit if we rushed around getting into debt all over the place. However, Alan's sister Linda phoned the day before Victoria was discharged and asked us to go and stay with them in Devon for a few days and we gratefully accepted.

The results of most of the tests had come through by the time Victoria was ready to leave and had all, thank God, shown that the disease had not so far spread anywhere else. The only result we were still waiting for was the bone scan which, I must admit, was the one that worried me the most, although I tried not to think about it too much. Also of course we had not had the results of the biopsy, but nor had we expected to at this stage.

As we made our farewells to the staff who had all been so kind, Sister Sarah promised they would let us know as soon as the results were through. There was of course no hint to Victoria that they would all be seeing her again quite soon.

There was however one slightly tense moment before we left. Victoria asked how long the stitches were to stay in her knee. We were at a loss for words, knowing that they would never be removed. Thankfully Jill, who was there at the time, was aware of our dilemma and replied quite calmly that they would remain for about ten days, which was true enough. Victoria would be seeing Mr Steel at that time when she would learn the reason that would make their removal unnecessary.

The events of the preceding few days still seemed hard to comprehend and like a very bad dream, with every chance (as we still hoped) that it might turn out not to be as bad as we had been told. But I think if we were totally honest with ourselves we would have realised that the most we could hope for now was that it had not spread to any other bones, that it had been caught in time.

We had a marvellously happy, albeit rather short stay in Devon. The weather was glorious, encouraging long walks in the beautiful countryside, golden and hazy, tinged with the first hint of Autumn in the early September sun. As we ambled along some country lane, it was not impossible to believe that everything was as it always had been, that nothing untoward had happened and we were just a normal happy family staying with relatives. Until one caught sight of Victoria in her wheelchair. Then the reality of the situation would come flooding back, the dread of what was to come. At the same time there was an almost dream-like quality about everything, making us feel that we only had to stay there forever and the awful truth would just disappear. Everything would be just as it had been six days ago. Six days! Was it really only six days since we had first been told? It felt like six years, the more so when one realised how much Victoria had been through in that short space of time—all the scans and tests and the biopsy. Yet she had borne it all without complaint and with a cheerfulness that had done a great deal to lift everyone else's spirits.

The short holiday came to an end all too quickly and it was hard to leave them all to come home, knowing what we were returning to. The girls were especially loath to leave their cousins. The distance that separated them prevented them seeing very much of each other. They had all thoroughly enjoyed their time together and their partings were not tinged with the sadness of ours. I think it was even harder for Linda and her husband Jim than it was for us. Perhaps they felt that living in Devon prevented them from being of any help to us. Also they had to come to terms with the fact that the next time they saw Victoria, she would only have one leg.

We told them, as we were to tell all our friends in the future, that although they might feel they could do nothing to help, in fact their support and comfort to us were invaluable. We could not have coped on our own. The knowledge that there was always someone to talk to, that one only had to pick up the phone, was a great support.

Every mile of the homeward journey brought the harsh reality of what was to come nearer and nearer. Trying not to think about it only seemed to make me dwell on it all the more, imagining all the time how Mr Steel would tell her and what might happen. It was her response to what he said that frightened me most. How would she react? It was too horrific in my mind. I tried to think about something else. What? All thought seemed to return again and again to the same focal point—next Thursday's appointment. It was the only thing at that moment that mattered. If only we could protect Victoria in some way from what she would have to know. We would have given anything for it to have been either of us instead.

After a few days at home we began to realise that we had to think positively about what was to happen. It would help no-one, least of all Victoria, who had to be our prime concern, for us to be continually full of self-pity and despair. We had by now been told the results of the bone scan and it too had proved clear. We started to accept the now inevitable fact that the amputation would be carried out.

We still had doubts though. Were we doing the right thing? Supposing we went ahead, only to discover perhaps a week or two later that the amputation could have been avoided? We had to be absolutely certain that there was no other option open to us. Plagued by these thoughts, we made arrangements to see our own doctor, who was very kind and patient with us but who nevertheless went on to explain that there was no other choice, even abroad. We only had one choice to preserve her life and that was the amputation.

I think we had both known this would be the case, but we had to be certain in our own minds. Perhaps it is all part of the process of learning to accept what you know in the end is unavoidable. Certainly after the visit we were able to talk about things in a much more positive way, considering what she would be able to continue to do, rather than what she would not. It was up to us, her parents, to help her as much as we could through what was bound to be a very traumatic experience.

# CHAPTER
## 4

Victoria was her usual cheerful self when we arrived at Mr Steel's clinic for her appointment. She liked and trusted him and didn't seem at all worried about going to see him. Though did she perhaps wonder about the outcome of today's visit?

The new school term had started the previous day, so we had dropped Joanna, rather reluctantly, before continuing on our way. There were times during the journey when I had felt that Victoria was rather quiet, as if she was thinking deeply, perhaps about that exploratory operation, the possibility that something was wrong with her knee. But she certainly gave no hint of any nervousness.

We were greeted at the entrance to the clinic by Sister Sarah from the children's ward and Mrs Page, the Social Worker. It was obvious to Alan and me that they were there to help us comfort Victoria, after she learned the truth of what was to happen. She, of course, found nothing strange in their being there and we left them chatting away like old friends as we went along the corridor to the Consultant's office.

As we entered, we could see that Victoria's file was on

the desk in front of him. We sat down and after the usual pleasantries he confirmed to us, referring to his notes now and again, that there was now no doubt. Victoria did have Osteogenic Sarcoma—a rare and virulent form of bone cancer. Her left leg would have to be amputated. The operation was scheduled to take place the following Monday 13 September—just four short days away.

We sat for what seemed an age with few words being spoken, as if we all wanted to put off the time when Victoria herself would have to be told. Although many people we had spoken to had assured us that we would be amazed at the way children seemed to accept something like this, I still felt that as they are all different, individual people; no-one could possibly predict how anyone else might react.

After confirming that we still wanted him to be the one to tell Victoria, Mr Steel asked me to bring her in. She looked up expectantly as I entered the room in which she had waited with her companions. 'He'd like to see you now,' I managed to say.

She jumped up immediately and preceded me out of the room, the wheelchair by now redundant. As I left the room Sarah said, 'We'll wait here for you,' reassuring me that we weren't on our own. I could think of nothing to say except to thank her vaguely, wishing we were all a million miles away. I caught up with Victoria.

'What did he say then?' she asked me. 'Is there something wrong?' Thankfully we had reached the door to Mr Steel's office. Coward that I was, I was spared from giving her a direct answer. Instead, I said, 'Well, we're here now, you'll be able to ask him yourself.'

My mind flashed back to that other appointment, just two weeks ago, when she had been told that there might be something wrong with her knee. The words she had spoken then seemed to ring in my ears as we entered the office. 'I thought he was going to tell me I had to have my leg cut off . . .'

Once we were all sitting down again, my heart was hammering against my ribs. Could no-one else hear it? Apparently not. Mr Steel was asking Victoria if she had had a nice holiday in Devon? Was the pain in her knee much worse?

'We had a smashing time and my knee hardly hurt at all,' she replied.

'Well, Victoria, I think you are probably sure by now that there is something wrong with your knee, aren't you?'

'Well, yes, I am,' she answered uncertainly, biting at her bottom lip. I reached out to hold her hand, as Alan had done.

'I'm afraid there is something quite seriously wrong,' he said. We had all felt that there was no point in beating about the bush. She had to know and he had to tell her. Had to tell her directly and in a way that she would understand exactly what was going to happen. 'In fact if we don't do something fairly quickly, it will spread to other parts of your body and will make you very ill indeed. So, to stop that from happening, I will have to take away the place in your bone where it is coming from.' He paused for a moment, leaning forward, and then continued, as if his words were for her alone, 'I'm going to ask you to be very brave.' She clutched our hands tighter. 'I'm afraid that to be able to stop it spreading any further, I will have to cut your leg off.' There was no other way to say it. He carried on without a pause to explain things more fully to her. But Alan and I

46

both stole a glance at her and were amazed to see that although one small tear had started on its way out of the corner of her eye, it was swiftly brushed away by the back of the hand she had withdrawn from mine. She seemed to take a deep breath as she returned her hand to its former position and continued to listen intently to what Mr Steel was saying.

Alan and I looked at one another, stunned. Had she heard? Understood what he had said? But she must have done, for she was now asking him if she would be able to run again after the amputation.

'I'm afraid I can't say that you will be able to run again but I can promise you that if you *really* want to do something, and you tell yourself you *can* do it, you will be able to do anything, and I'm sure you will.'

She looked pleased at his last words. I was so glad we had asked him to tell her. He was so good with her and was able to explain it all so much better than we could have done, using words that she could understand. Still, we could not quite believe the way in which she was taking it. The least we had expected were floods of tears and here she was really putting us to shame in the way she was accepting it all so stoically. Perhaps the reaction would come later on.

He went on to explain to us that we would be able to go to the limb fitting centre at Roehampton Hospital tomorrow, to meet the people who would eventually make and fit her artificial leg and teach her to walk again. I must admit that Alan and I had both been rather shocked at the suddenness of this, but were to realise later that it was as much to bring home to Victoria the full implication of what was about to happen as anything else.

Yet again Victoria proved how much more sensible she was being about the whole thing, as she asked him what her new leg would be like? And then, 'Will I be able to swim with it?' This caused us all to smile a little as Mr Steel answered her, 'Not actually with it on. I think that might damage it slightly!' She giggled at this. 'But you will be able to swim perfectly well with one leg. I've got one young patient who lost his leg in a motorcycle accident, and apart from swimming he also plays football. I think he finds the artificial leg quite useful for getting rid of the opposition!' This all eased the tension. On a more serious note he added, 'He is also riding his motorcycle again, although I'm not really sure that I approve of that.' He also briefly touched on the fact that she might have some treatment, called radiotherapy, in case some of the cells had broken away, but she would know more about that after the operation.

'Have I got cancer?' she asked, in a quite calm and matter-of-fact way. We were all of us astounded. Where had she got that idea from? It was true. But how did she know? 'Yes, it is a form of cancer, but it can be cured, you mustn't worry about it,' Mr Steel managed to say.

'Oh, I'm not worried,' she said.

I was still in a daze as we sorted out all the dates and times for the various appointments and visits. As we were about to leave Mr Steel came round from behind his desk, and putting his hands on her shoulders said, 'I think you're absolutely marvellous, Victoria. You are a very brave little girl. And I'm sure you will be able to do anything you want to later on and I'm also sure you will do it very well.'

She lowered her head, slightly embarrassed by his words, not knowing quite what to say. We said goodbye

Victoria and Demelza visit Sefton before the big parade
(*Daily Mail*)

At home, May 1983 (*Daily Express*)

Victoria riding her bicycle after the amputation. She won the medal she is wearing in the school gymnastics display (*Daily Express*)

Joanna and Victoria on their way to school

to him—for the time being at least.

As we made our way back to the room in which Sarah and Mrs Page were waiting for us, Victoria suddenly said, in a voice tinged with what I felt was relief, 'Why didn't you tell me it was only that? I wouldn't have minded. I knew there was something wrong.'

'Well,' Alan said, 'we thought it better if Mr Steel told you himself. What did you think he was going to say?'

'I thought he was going to tell me I was going to die.'

Completely at a loss for words, all we could do was reach down and put our arms around her, humbled by the fact that she was taking it so well compared with the way we had reacted. She was, after all, the 'victim'.

Sarah and Mrs Page were visibly surprised by her demeanour. As we made our way upstairs to the ward for a cup of much needed coffee, Mrs Page said to me, 'Well, it obviously hasn't sunk in yet, shock sometimes does that. She couldn't have understood what he was saying.'

'I think you're wrong about that,' I replied. 'She understands exactly what is going to happen. You should have heard the questions she was asking him. They were not the sort of questions that a person who hadn't taken things in would have asked.'

I told her what had been said. Especially what Victoria had only just said to Alan and me. 'Well, it certainly is amazing, but there may be more of a reaction later on, when she has had time to think about it all more fully.'

I felt she was totally wrong in her assessment. Victoria had completely understood what she had been told, had accepted the fact that her leg had to be amputated, but I kept my thoughts to myself.

I think that Victoria's strength lay in the fact that she knew exactly what was going to happen and why: the fact that if the amputation did not go ahead she would become very ill indeed. It was almost as if she had decided that there was no point in dwelling on the negative aspects of only having one leg. She felt she would still be better off than many people and she just wanted to get on with her life as normally as possible. Her attitude to what she was going through was to become even more apparent as the day passed. There were never any doubts as far as we were concerned that she did not realise the full implications of what was to happen.

As we sat in Sister Sarah's office, it was she who asked Victoria if there was anything else she wanted to know, something that she had perhaps not liked to ask Mr Steel himself. She thought for a moment before replying, quite calmly, 'What will happen to my leg, after it's been cut off?'

Sarah did not seem in the least perturbed by this question. I could never have imagined asking such a thing myself, much as I might have wanted to know. I couldn't help darting a glance at Mrs Page. Was that the question of a child who hadn't taken things in?

Sarah replied to the question she had been asked. 'Your leg will be taken to the laboratory, where it can be examined thoroughly, then they may be able to find out more about what caused it all.'

'So that other children might not have to have the same thing done?' said Victoria.

'Well, that's what they are hoping for, one day,' replied Sarah.

'Well, I'm glad my leg might be able to help.'

Victoria asked one or two other questions, such as how long she would be in hospital and how long the operation

50

might take. She was so cheerful but must have really worried underneath her calm exterior that she was going to die. Compared with that, she felt that having a leg amputated was nothing to worry about.

During the homeward journey, Victoria made plain her wish that she should be the one to tell other people what was to happen to her leg.

'Granny will be in a bit of a state, won't she?' she said, 'and Nannie.' (This is the name Alan's mother is known by to her grandchildren.)

'Well—they did know that it might have to happen,' I told her.

'Does everyone know? I wanted to tell them myself.'

We explained that it was only the immediate family, apart from Joanna, who knew anything at all.

'Well, I want to tell Joanna. If I come to school with you when you pick her up, I can tell all my friends too. Perhaps Granny and Nannie won't be too upset if I tell them myself. After all, there are a lot of people much worse off than me.'

I suppose we had not really thought of it like that, until she herself pointed it out. I still found it difficult to see in those terms, but it was a strange and humbling experience to have things put into perspective by the very one who was the subject of our concern. So it was that she began astounding others with the calm way in which she told them what was to happen, a way which in itself caused one or two rather heart-stopping moments. The first of these was when we collected Joanna from school. Victoria had told several of her classmates, those who were her special friends. As we were driving off afterwards, I was disturbed to see one of her best friends in floods of tears. This was made even more worrying by the fact that the child in question was a weekly boarder at the school and would not even be able to share her grief with her own mother until the next day. I was extremely relieved to see that one of the Sisters stopped to talk to her and took her inside the school.

We had been to see the Headmistress the previous week to explain things to her. She was a great source of strength and inspiration to us both. We knew that she and all the other staff would help any of the other children, particularly those in the same classes as our two girls, who were in any way disturbed by Victoria's illness. Then came the time to tell Joanna. I suppose it might have been done with a little more finesse, but children are very forthright anyway and it was probably better for Victoria to tell her herself. Almost as soon as we had driven out of the school gates, we heard Victoria's voice as she said, 'Now Joanna, I've got something to tell you and it might be a bit of a shock, but you'll just have to be brave. I've got to have my leg cut off.'

Joanna started to cry. 'No, Victoria. Why?' she sobbed.

'You mustn't cry, because I've got to have it done. If I don't, it will spread from my knee and get much worse. It's much better to lose a leg than to die, isn't it?'

Joanna nodded rather uncertainly and managed to brush away the tears and stop crying. Victoria had put her arm round her in a sisterly way and given her a hug. I told Joanna how brave Victoria had been and that we all had to be, although it wasn't easy.

Joanna seemed to have calmed down somewhat when Victoria suddenly said to her, 'Do you want to know what is going to happen to my leg, after it's cut off?'

She nodded silently, but I could see that she was none

too sure about whether she did or not. Perhaps it would be better if Victoria did tell her? Too late to do anything now. I listened in disbelief as Victoria in all seriousness but with a mischievous twinkle in her eyes said, 'Well, I'm going to bring it home and put it on the shelf in my bedroom!'

'Really Victoria, that's not a very nice thing to have told her,' I answered rather sharply. Joanna's face was turned to her sister in horror. 'Don't worry Joanna, she's only joking,' I said, glaring at Victoria, who was still laughing but went on to tell Joanna what was really going to happen to her leg.

There was one rather anxious moment when we stopped at the village shops on the way home. I had gone into the greengrocer's and the girls had both gone into the sweet shop. When I returned to the car, Alan said, 'I think you'd better go and have a word with Mrs Cooper. Victoria has just told her about the operation and she came out of the shop in floods of tears.'

'What did you say, Victoria?' I asked, wondering what on earth had made the poor woman break down.

'I just told her that I was going to have my leg cut off.'

She said it as if she was going to have her hair cut. Her bluntness was quite amazing, but I could see that it might cause problems if this afternoon was anything to go by. I spoke to Mrs Cooper and she explained that it was more Victoria's attitude to the whole thing that had surprised her and caused the tears.

'Does she really understand what is going to happen?' she asked.

'Yes, she does.' I could see that she was not sure whether to believe me or not, but at least she was in a calmer frame of mind than she had been half an hour before.

We tried to explain to Victoria later that evening that not everyone was going to be as brave as she was about the operation. But it was an uphill task, she simply could not see why it upset others so much. It was to happen to her anyway, and if the leg was not amputated, it would endanger her life. It all seemed so obvious to her and she reiterated the fact that there were others worse off than she.

How could we, who having felt so dejected and unhappy for nearly two weeks, live up to the example she was now setting us? It was going to be extremely difficult. Many people said to us that perhaps she did not understand the full implication of what was to happen and all that it would entail. But with the questions she had asked and the way she talked about things, we were certain that she did. Surely if she had not been fully aware there would have been some sort of breakdown? Some loss of composure? But there never was. Never once did she stoop to self-pity as we had.

Both my mother and Alan's had managed to keep fairly calm when she had broken the news to them. Although they had known about the possibility and had had time to begin to accept the inevitable, I think they both hoped (as indeed we all had) that the amputation would, in the end, be unnecessary. They took it very well. How could they do otherwise, when Victoria herself was so accepting of the situation? They had both coped with it in different ways. My own mother had floored us all by her attitude, in view of the fact that we had thought she was the one person most likely to go to pieces over it. But Victoria used to talk to her quite a lot about it all and Mum always remembers her saying, 'Don't worry about me Gran, I'll be all right.'

Although Alan's mother spoke about it a little to Alan, she rarely mentioned it to me and we both had the impression that she felt that if she did not talk about it and ignored it, the situation would just go away. I don't think she really believed that the amputation would take place. It all showed us how each individual has his own way of coping with a given situation.

Joanna seemed to have accepted the situation with almost as much stoicism as Victoria, although I think that at the age of only seven she could hardly grasp any of the implications that might arise. She was always wanting to buy little presents for Victoria and through everything that followed never for one moment displayed the slightest sign of jealousy. As she told me one evening when I put her to bed, 'I just want Victoria to get better, Mummy.'

Alan and I had always been close and had a good marriage. Any difficulties we might have had (what married couple has not?) seemed only to have strengthened our relationship rather than driven us apart. What we were going through now underlined this and helped us through a very trying period in our lives, happy in the knowledge that we always had each other for support. Naturally we were not in complete agreement over every little detail. I was always the more pessimistic when it came to speculating on how Victoria would cope with life after the amputation, more concerned as to how she would be treated by others, but then I'm a pessimist by nature. But we were always able to discuss the issues rationally and, in the best interests of all concerned, we certainly never argued over anything. People have asked how Victoria's illness affected our marriage: I can honestly say that it didn't, except, as I've said, to bring us even closer. It was something that affected both of us equally, and it wasn't our best interests we had at heart, but Victoria's. We couldn't let her down.

Both of us wondered, however, whether the coming visit to Roehampton might have more of an effect on Victoria's attitude. She still had both her legs. How would she react to seeing others who were without a limb? Again we waited for the tears that never came, for some sign that she was depressed or upset. But there was none.

Alan and I found the limb fitting centre depressing, sitting in the waiting room among the other, mainly elderly, amputees, with artificial limbs lying by their sides. Some were contained in very large and obvious brown paper bags, but many were just lying on the floor, unwrapped.

The Consultant who was dealing with Victoria was very kind and considerate and introduced us to the man who would eventually make and fit Victoria's leg. She was thrilled to discover that as an apprentice he had actually worked on the limbs that had been dropped to World War Two fighter pilot Sir Douglas Bader, when he had been a prisoner of war in Germany.

We were shown the type of limb she would be fitted with, which turned out to be as unlike anything we had imagined as possible, having an ankle as well as a knee 'joint' and being covered in a very fine type of foam rubber, giving it a very lifelike appearance. It was one of the latest designs, still a prototype in fact. We learned later that Victoria was the youngest patient at that time to have used it.

I was a little shocked and wondered whether Victoria might be too when they began to take her measurements, her height and the length of her legs. I was again put to shame by the fact that she seemed totally unconcerned. It was explained to her that this would help speed things up a bit when the time came. And her main concern, after all, was getting back to normal afterwards.

Of course there was not much that could be done until after the operation, when they would be able to make a plaster cast just from her waist down to the top of her thigh. This would be used to make what I can only describe as a sort of corset. It would be made from a supple form of plastic and would be moulded to fit her bottom. This would be strapped around her hips with heavy duty Velcro fastening. The artificial limb would be attached to this, meaning that she would have to use her hips, the weight of her body being taken by her own leg, to throw the artificial leg forward and so walk. She would have nothing left of her own leg, no 'stump' to speak of, to help her.

To prevent any spread of the cancer, her femur was to be removed, leaving her with just the hip bone on her left side. The cancer was known already to be affecting the bottom third of the femur and was certainly beginning to spread to other parts of the bone. Therefore, to be on the side of safety, the whole bone would be removed.

There was not much time left now before the operation was due to take place. Perhaps it was better not to have too long to wait. We just had enough time to buy Victoria the one or two extra things she would need for her coming stay in hospital. I wondered if Joanna might be a little jealous of the fact that it was Victoria who was being bought all the new nightclothes and smart sponge bag. I had always previously bought things for each of them at the same time. But never once was there any protest or talk of this not being fair. Joanna seemed to understand and accept it all in a very adult way. She had always been very much the baby of the family, yet with all that had happened she seemed to have grown up almost overnight. She was always wanting to do things to help, which she had never done before. It was Victoria who insisted that Joanna should have some little present and bought her one herself.

So, with her new things and one or two toys and games neatly packed in her bag, she was ready to leave for the hospital. We left home just after lunch on the Sunday, the day prior to the operation.

I couldn't help thinking as I watched her walking down the path to the car that this time tomorrow it would all be over. Victoria would only have one leg. Nor could I help asking myself how she could possibly have such a dreadful and life threatening disease when there were no visible signs? Apart from the stitches from the biopsy, her legs seemed so normal, just like any other child's. I could hardly drag my eyes away from them, couldn't take in that although there was no outward sign the evidence was most certainly there, hidden in the bone. But anyone looking at her who did not know, could never have guessed that there was anything wrong at all.

# CHAPTER
## 5

Now, on entering the children's ward, it was like coming home. One immediately felt safe and somehow cocooned from the outside world. All the nurses we had met on the previous visit were there to welcome us and of course they made a great fuss of Victoria and Joanna too. They were always very good about including Joanna in what was going on as much as possible.

We had both realised that Victoria might ask one of us to stay overnight at the hospital this time, and indeed she did. Consequently, we were shown into one of the smaller twin bedded rooms that were kept especially for such a purpose. I was going to stay for this, the first night, before the operation, after which we felt we would both want to stay for a couple of nights. Thereafter, we stayed on alternate nights. We had Joanna to consider too, and did not want her to feel alone at such a worrying time, or excluded in any way. She would be spending the next few days with Alan's parents, as would my mother, although my sister had had to return to her job the previous weekend. Joanna always looked forward to a stay at Nannie's. Nannie was never without a plentiful supply of sweets and would also take and collect her from school. My own mother did not drive any more, which was one of the reasons for them both going to stay with Mum and Dad Hart.

The usual weight and temperature checks were soon completed. Then Victoria was asked if she would like to have a bath.

'But I had one last night,' she replied indignantly. 'You're mad on washing in here. Can't I have one later? I wanted to go to the playroom with Joanna, before she has to go home.'

I should have realised that this was the reason for her reluctance, and of course no objections were raised as long as she promised to have a bath later on. It was explained to her how necessary it was before any operation. I said that I would make sure that she had one later.

The nurses had commandeered one of the few colour television sets for Victoria; not that she would be able to watch it very much during the next few days, but it made her feel at home. We left Alan ensconced on the smaller of the two beds, watching the Sunday afternoon football, as we went to the playroom. Victoria muttered something about 'not even being able to get away from the wretched football in here,' then, giggling, 'Still, it makes it seem more like home.'

The time seemed to pass fairly quickly and soon we had to return to her room. Her supper had arrived. She said she was not hungry, but she managed to eat a little. The remainder was wolfed down by Joanna, who was always hungry.

When at last the much postponed bath had taken place, it was getting quite late and time for Alan to take Joanna home. She would not be staying with Nannie until the following night. We felt it would be less traumatic for her if Alan took her to school the first morning, less upsetting for her than if she had suddenly been left without either of us. She did not really want to leave Victoria, as if she too realised it would be different the next time she saw her. I had to fight back the tears as I watched them hugging each other and saying goodbye, thinking that although they might argue quite viciously at times, they really were very close and very fond of each other.

As soon as Victoria was settled in bed, watching 'her own', as she called it, television, I went down to the staff canteen for something to eat, although I must say I didn't feel much like eating anything, as if the food might choke me. I still couldn't get used to what was going to happen but I would just have to.

After I returned to the room, the nurses popped in and out during the evening to see if Victoria was all right. Would she like a cup of tea? She was told that if she had any trouble in getting to sleep, she only had to ask and they would give her something to help her. She accepted the tea, but declined anything else.

Later in the evening, we were both surprised and pleased when Mr Steel came in to see her. I thought it particularly kind of him as, being a Sunday, I was sure he would not have been on duty and must have made a special journey from his home. He was so kind and concerned, saying that he hoped Victoria wasn't worrying too much about tomorrow, hoping that she would get a good night's rest.

As he left, he turned towards her by the door to say, 'You know Victoria, you really are marvellous. I'll see you tomorrow.' It was almost as if he could hardly believe (himself) how she was taking it. Then he left.

When the door had closed Victoria asked me why he kept saying nice things about her, because it made her feel embarrassed and she didn't know how to answer him.

'I don't think he expects you to say anything. It's just that everyone thought you would be terribly upset when you found out about your leg. We are all very proud of the way you have been so brave, you know,' I said, 'and Mr Steel just wants you to know that. Daddy and I do too, we both love you very much.'

She looked so beautiful, especially when she smiled, as she did now. She reached out her arms to me and gave me a big hug, telling me again not to worry. 'I'll be all right, you know.'

She said she was feeling a little sleepy now, so I switched off the TV and the lights, although there was still a night light. No doubt we would be disturbed at the crack of dawn in the morning, so an early night would do me good as well. I was surprised how easily I too fell asleep, and how quickly what I had thought would be a long and tedious night passed.

We were woken by one of the night staff, as I had thought, fairly early. Well, it seemed like it to me anyway. I was brought a cup of tea, which was very welcome. Victoria, of course, could have nothing now and I noticed that her bottle of squash had been removed from the top of the locker and a notice placed above the bed bearing the words NIL BY MOUTH. Things that go bump in the night!

Shortly after I had returned from breakfast, Dr Jones, Mr Steel's houseman, came into the room to take a blood sample. Victoria liked this personable young man and was very pleased to see him again. She was not so pleased about the reason for his visit, but as usual did not complain. The need for any artwork on her leg was this time rendered unnecessary by the stitches left in after the biopsy. One of the things she had said, when told about the amputation, had been, 'At least I won't have to have the stitches taken out.'

She was now free for a few hours at least to spend some time in the playroom or to draw, until it was time for her pre-op. injection. The operation was not due to take place until two o'clock. As Alan would soon be with us, she decided to stay in her room and draw. 'He might not be able to find us,' she had said. But I think she just wanted us all to be together, without other people around. She had brought all her felt tipped pens and was soon amusing the staff with her caricatures of them.

Shortly after midday one of the staff nurses, a nice girl called Anne, came into the room accompanied by a second year student. In her hand she carried the tray bearing the dreaded pre-op. injection. Victoria looked at it with digust, at the same time knowing that it had to be done. However, she made no fuss and soon settled down to dose fitfully as the injection took effect. Alan and I sat by her bed in silence, just watching her as she slept. Still I could hardly grasp that this was really happening. But it was, nothing could change the outcome now.

The seconds ticked away. Alan and I glanced at the clock, almost simultaneously. One thirty. They would soon be here to wheel her down to the operating theatre. I looked again to the bed where Victoria was drowsing contentedly, opening her eyes only now and then as if to reassure herself that we were both still there by her side. My eyes were drawn again and again to the shape her legs made beneath the sheets, the shape of two legs. In such a short time she would appear different. How would she look? I still found it hard to grasp that in just a few short hours she would have only one leg.

The porter entered with Staff Nurse Jill. Victoria woke up, pleased to see that her favourite nurse would be the one to accompany her to the theatre. Alan and I both kissed her and, not knowing quite what to say, said nothing. This was it then, there was no going back now. As we stood in the corridor and watched her bed disappearing round the corner, the reality seemed to hit us anew. We just put our arms round each other and cried.

# CHAPTER
## 6

They were wheeling her bed into the empty space awaiting it in the high-dependency room of the children's ward, thus called because it was situated opposite the nurses. It was the room in which Victoria had been during her first stay. One of the theatre nurses had come up with her, as there were various tubes and an intravenous drip to be contended with. She was covered with several blankets, but the signs that the operation had been carried out were all too visible. Why should I have thought otherwise?

She slept for most of the rest of that day and the next, from the effects of the anaesthetic and the pain-killing drugs. Alan and I spent most of the time during those first few days by her bedside. We didn't say very much to each other, but we thought volumes. We each seemed to be in tune with what the other was thinking. There was no need for words.

Two days after the operation the pain-killing injections ceased—as much by Victoria's demand as anything else. She hated those needles. She seemed much more like her old self again, and was looking forward to Joanna's visit later in the day, as we were, not having seen our younger daughter for a couple of days now. She had even expressed the wish to watch television, so things were beginning to look up.

Then suddenly and without warning, Victoria gave a scream as her body contorted in a paroxysm of pain. What on earth was wrong? Had something gone wrong? I immediately asked what the matter was as Alan pressed the buzzer to call a nurse. We felt so helpless.

'It's my leg,' she gasped, 'I thought they were going to cut if off. Why haven't they?'

'But they have darling,' was all I could reply. What had made her think that? A staff nurse had arrived at her bedside and explained to us that these were phantom pains. It was to do with the nerves that had been severed yet were still sending messages to the brain. I had heard that this could happen but had not really expected it in Victoria's case, as she was so young.

'But why does it still hurt so much? It's just as bad as it was before. It's terrible in my foot too.'

'It's because the nerves that were in your leg haven't got used to it's not being there yet,' the nurse explained to her. 'I'll get you something for the pain.'

'Not an injection. I don't want an injection,' came the little voice from the bed. She would sooner put up with a great deal of pain rather than suffer an injection.

'There's no need to worry about that, you can't have any more injections at the moment after all you've had. It will be tablets. Will that be OK? Can you swallow them all right?'

She nodded silently. The pain still clearly visible in her eyes. How I wished I could make it go away and not come back. For we knew it might return again, as bad as ever, once the effects of the drugs (usually Valium) had worn off. The pains did last for several days and all we could do was to sit and hold her hand as she writhed on the bed in obvious agony, until the drugs took control. The pains were not continuous and there would be long periods in between the bouts of pain, when she showed no sign of the distress they caused her. She never let them get her down.

Several days after the first attack, the extreme pain was replaced to some extent by itchiness! She was highly amused (and we were amazed) when a staff nurse who had experience of nursing older amputees was able to relieve the itching by scratching the air where the foot and leg would have been. I too tried this technique on one or two occasions, without much success. In fact I was told I was useless. It seems there must be a certain knack to it. It hardly seemed conceivable that Victoria was still able to feel these sensations in a leg that was no longer there, but having spoken to doctors and nurses and former patients, we had to accept the reality of this phenomenon.

Thankfully when Joanna came in to see her sister, it was during a time when she was free from pain. She hated others to see her in agony, mainly because she knew it was upsetting for them. Particularly for her grandparents. She did not like to see them upset, feeling responsible. We did occasionally have to have a few quiet words with them and we had to guess when Victoria was in any pain and ask them to leave if we felt it was becoming a strain for her to control. One of the worst things for Victoria was someone coming to see her and leaning over her in bed saying, 'Oh, you do look well.' This did happen once or twice. She said to me after the first occasion, 'Why did they say that? I'm not ill. I'm better now, that's why I had my leg taken off.' When you think of it, there can be little worse for a child than having some adult say things like that.

Just four days after the operation Victoria was paid a visit by the Physiotherapist who worked with Mr Steel. She arrived at the bedside armed with a pair of crutches and a walking frame. Good grief, I thought, they surely won't get her up already?

'Hello, Victoria. Remember me? I'm Sally.' We had met her the day we saw Mr Steel.

'I'm just going to hide these crutches behind the curtain, next to your bed. I think they will be just the right size for you and we don't want anyone else to sneak off with them, do we?'

As she did so, Victoria struggled to sit up further in her bed, her eyes alight with interest at this new turn of events.

'What's that?' she asked, pointing to the frame.

'That's a walking frame. It's the same as the ones we give to elderly people who can't walk steadily. You won't be able to use the crutches for a bit, so I'll get you started with the frame, just to get you standing properly and get your balance back.'

Before any of us could stop her, the bed clothes were being thrown back and she was trying eagerly to get out of bed.

'Well, I didn't mean right now, I thought perhaps tomorrow,' said Sally, slightly taken aback. 'But I suppose it will be all right, if you feel up to it?' Victoria's expression was enough for anyone to guess what she wanted to do.

'You may feel rather dizzy at first, so you must tell me if

you feel at all faint? Otherwise I'll have Mr Steel after me for maltreating his patients.'

Sally helped Victoria to stand up and placed the frame in front of her. I held my breath. In no time at all, she was standing with only the frame for support, apparently full of confidence and her balance seemed to me to be unaffected. Even Sally was surprised by this. It was usual, she said, after an amputation such as Victoria had undergone, for the hip to drop down, as there was now no leg to support it.

'Can I try a few steps?' she asked, already starting to move the frame forward.

'It's best not to overdo things to start with,' said Sally.

'I won't, but please just let me try?'

'Go on then, but I hope you won't feel faint.'

It did not take her long to work out how she had to move the frame first and then her foot to catch up with it. We stood by amazed, as she walked to the end of the bed and back again. She wouldn't have stopped then if Sally hadn't insisted that she did so and promised that she could have another go tomorrow. That was our first insight into the fact that Victoria would never treat what had happened to her as a disability. Nor did she want any sympathy. She just wanted to get on with life, to get walking again and to get back to school. The quicker she could start to achieve this the better.

Exactly one week after the operation it was time for her first appointment at another part of the district hospital, situated on the other side of the town, where all cancer treatment is carried out. This meant a short ambulance trip to reach our destination, which Victoria found quite exciting after the confines of the hospital ward. She would be starting the prescribed course of radiotherapy at the end of the week, as soon as a 'shield', to protect areas of tissue surrounding the lungs, had been prepared. This was the reason for that day's visit.

We travelled armed with pain-killers. The pain was still quite severe, but seemed to attack at less frequent intervals. The process of constructing the 'shield' was a fairly lengthy one, and we couldn't be sure exactly when the next bout of pain might occur. The process involved a machine exactly like the one that would be used for the treatment itself, called a simulator. Through this X-ray pictures would be shown on a screen, from which measurements of the lungs could be taken. From these the shield would be made from polystyrene filled with lead, ensuring protection of the tissue.

It was the first of several visits we made before the shield was completed and the treatment could begin. Interspersed with these were daily trips along the corridor outside the children's ward to the physiotherapy room, for some practice in walking before the crutches were used. She was started off by walking up and down between parallel bars, and, as she became more proficient, she began to use the crutches. After only a few days she was walking up and down steps and ramps, to get used to going on different levels. She became so good that there were times when we had difficulty in keeping up with the pace she set.

One or two people voiced the opinion that she might become so used to getting around on her crutches, she wouldn't want to give them up in favour of her artificial limb when the time came. She would be able to move that bit faster with the crutches, to start with at least. But Alan and I never thought that. We knew that she was just preparing for that time, which could not come too quickly for her. Hardly a day passed without some reference to it.

The treatment, once started, was to continue daily, except for weekends. There had been no side effects, apart from feeling a little more tired than usual. This though could be put down to all the walking practice, as much as anything else.

She was already two or three days into the course of treatment when the time came for the eagerly awaited visit to Roehampton, for the plaster cast to be taken. This had not been possible until all the stitches from the wound had been removed. She was slightly nervous as to what the taking of the cast would entail. She had never had cause to come into contact with plaster casts until now. To set her mind at rest and to show her that it would not be a painful experience, Sally suggested that she made a cast of Victoria's wrist. It would be a little bit of fun too. The task was accomplished with a little mess and even more laughter. When it had dried and had been removed, Victoria asked if she might keep it.

'Yes, of course you can, but they do get a bit messy after a while and tend to start crumbling,' said Sally.

'Oh, that's all right, I just want to put it on when Nannie comes in to see me. She'll think I've broken my wrist as well. I can't wait to see her face!' She was a little devil, but we were only too pleased that she hadn't lost her sense of fun.

'You are a monkey,' said Sally, in mock horror, 'I hope she doesn't get too much of a shock.'

I did wonder what Victoria was going to get up to next. Only the previous day, on our return to the ward after lunch, Victoria had been nowhere to be found. No-one seemed to know where she was, although I did think some of the staff wore rather knowing looks. Sister came over to where Alan and I were standing and said that there was a telephone call for me. I wondered who would possibly contact me here. Hoping that nothing untoward had happened to Joanna at school, I took the call. The reply to my brief hello, was a voice I recognised only too well.

'Hello Mummy, did you wonder where I was? Well I'm shopping . . . in Debenhams!'

'What!' I exclaimed, aghast at the prospect. The store was situated at least two miles away in the centre of the town. 'You can't be.'

'I am, Sue brought me.' Sue was one of the auxiliaries whom she had taken quite a shine to, but I couldn't believe that she would have been allowed to take Victoria shopping in the town, although she had been pestering everyone for days to let her go. She seemed to have a particular yen to go to Debenhams for some reason.

'Now come on, where are you really? I know you can't be in the town.'

'I am really shopping. I'll bring you something back, see you later.' With that she hung up.

Of course, a few minutes later the ward doors opened to reveal Victoria with a huge grin on her face, pleased that she had fooled me, even for so short a time. She had indeed been shopping as it turned out. The League of Friends of the hospital ran a small shop in the foyer of the hospital, selling confectionery and small toiletries. That was where she had been and of course had used the public telephone next to it to phone the ward. There was also the time when the slightly more mischievous side of her nature came through. A young boy had been brought into the ward, with a broken arm, which was causing him some distress. His distress became even more apparent when the word injection was mentioned. Victoria's mirth increased and a wicked grin began to spread from ear to ear, as she listened to the howls issuing from behind the closed curtains. She hated all thought of injections and needles, and she was making the most of someone else's discomfort. As the nurse entered bearing the tray containing the dreaded syringe, the howls increased, accompanied now with a certain amount of thrashing about on the bed.

'Well, if you won't let me do it, I shall have to get the doctor,' came the voice of one of the nurses, who stood for no nonsense from her young charges.

I was horrified when Victoria, in a voice which I felt sure would be heard through the thin curtains, said, 'Go on Mary, stick it in him.'

'Victoria, that's a horrid thing to say, it would be different if it was you.' I tried to admonish her, but she thought it was great entertainment.

The smile was soon wiped off her face, however, when Dr Jones who had in the end been called, popped his head round the curtain, and, turning to the nurse, said, 'Isn't it time for this young lady to have her injection now?' Victoria soon realised that they didn't miss a thing, and she was never quite so quick to make fun at the expense of others again.

It was Alan who drove her up to Roehampton. We even drove her to the other hospital for her treatment now, which saved waiting about for hours for ambulances which often had to make long trips to pick up other patients as well.

We felt there was no point in us both going to

Roehampton: Victoria was quite happy to be on her own with her Dad for a change. They had always been very close, and she liked nothing better than to have her Daddy all to herself. The events of the past few weeks had certainly made Alan feel so much more protective towards her, although he never spoiled her. He was lucky too in that working for his father he was able to have the time off, and could spend as much time as possible with her, something he really appreciated, especially as we both realised that for the majority of fathers this might not have been so easy.

By all accounts the afternoon had gone very well, although Victoria had found it rather boring, as she had to stand for what seemed to her, anyway, hours in a support frame, while the plaster cast was being made. It had to harden off slightly before it was removed, to maintain the correct shape. This, of course, could not have been done without the prior removal of the stitches a few days earlier, about twelve days after the amputation had taken place.

The highlight of the day had been a visit to Hampton Court which she had greatly enjoyed, as they had been learning all about King Henry VIII at school the previous term in history lessons. The greatest talking point was that they had got lost in the maze — very exciting, she might not be able to get back to the hospital! They had taken the wheelchair, as it might have proved too tiring for Victoria, with everything else she had to contend with. In fact, it was to prove rather more tiring for Alan, who had to push her through the maze, although he always maintained he had known the way out all along. Compared to all their goings on I had experienced a rather mundane day of household chores that had been allowed to slip rather badly over the last few weeks.

A few days later we were given the best surprise of all when Jill came into the room (Victoria was by now back in the original room with two beds). She asked Victoria, 'How would you like to go home?'

'Ooh, yes please, do I have to come back on Sunday night?' Today was Friday, but we had been allowed to take her out for a picnic the previous weekend.

'No, I mean home to stay. You're getting around so well now, the doctors think you'll be better off at home.' Jill then added, 'Besides, you'll have us all worn out soon, we can't keep up with you any more!'

There is no need for me to describe how thrilled we all were at this prospect, especially Victoria. It was all so completely unexpected, even to Alan and myself. We began collecting together all her accumulated belongings, the dozens of cards she had received, her appointment card for a checkup in a few weeks' time. In under an hour we were ready to leave.

In a strange way, even for Alan and me, it felt a little like leaving home. We had spent so much time there and become so involved with the daily routine of hospital life. I could easily see how quickly one might become institutionalised. It felt most strange to go out through the hospital doors, knowing that we would not have to return tomorrow, although for the next week Victoria would still have to come in daily for the radiotherapy treatment.

We bade a fond farewell to as many of the staff as were on duty that day, promising that we would visit them whenever we were in town. We could never thank them enough for all they had done, helping us through a very difficult period in our lives, one that I'm sure would have been even more difficult without their kind help and understanding. They had made us feel that nothing had to be faced alone; we could count on their support.

# CHAPTER
## 7

'It's fabulous to be back home,' Victoria said, as we settled round the fire later that evening. 'I'd forgotten what it was like. I really missed being here, you know. It felt a bit strange at first, it seems as if I've been away for ages.'

'It's lovely for us too, to have you back home,' said Alan. And then voicing my own thoughts, 'It's just a shame that the new house isn't quite ready. It would have been much nicer if we could have really taken you home.'

'I don't mind. I just want to be with all of you. It doesn't matter where we are.' She had really done a lot of growing up over the past few weeks. Perhaps we all had.

It was hardly surprising that the new house wasn't ready as we had originally hoped by the end of September. Alan had spent so much time at the hospital, and I, for one, could certainly not have coped with everything without his help, even if it did mean that the move would now have to be postponed until the end of October. I'm sure Victoria felt the same, but it was enough for her just to be with us again. As it was already the last week of September, we would not have too long to wait.

Now we felt like a complete family again. How long was it since we had last all been together like this in the evening? At least now we could settle down to some form of normality, although Victoria was unable to return to school, despite desperately wanting to, before she had her artificial leg.

The radiotherapy treatment had run its course. The next visit to Roehampton would not be until early November, by which time her limb would be ready. Alan had returned to work as well, which meant that all going well we should be able to move in at the end of October.

I thought Victoria might become more than a little bored being at home with me all day, with nothing much going on and none of the distractions of a busy hospital ward. But she was quite happy. She had always been content with her own company, liking nothing better than to be able to draw and to write stories.

One thing, however, she enjoyed greatly. It involved spending money—not vast sums I admit. She loved to come up to the little parade of shops not too far from the house and spend her pocket money. She also had some school work to do, much to her disgust. I had been to see her class teacher to ask if she might have some English and Mathematics to do at home. Once Victoria realised that if she fell too far behind the other girls in her class it would be even more difficult to catch up, she got down to doing a little each day without too much complaint.

As well as school work she had a great many thank you letters to write. In addition to all the cards, she had received a large quantity of presents, many from people we hardly knew, and they were still arriving daily. The week following her return home brought one card in particular. It was to have special meaning, not just for Victoria, but for all of us, in the months that followed. It read simply, 'I hope you are getting on well and perhaps when you are better, you can ask your Mummy to bring you along to see me at the barracks—SEFTON.' Several kisses concluded the message.

There can be few who have not heard of this brave Household Cavalry horse, who had recovered from such terrible injuries inflicted during an IRA bomb attack in Hyde Park the previous July. As fate would have it it was on the very day that Victoria's birthday treat had taken place (although it was not her actual birthday).

Victoria, needless to say, was absolutely thrilled to bits to receive such a card, and hardly able to believe her eyes, she said, 'Can we really go and see him?'

'Yes, of course you can. You'll have to write back straight away and thank him and say that you would love to go.'

Alan and I had known of the possibility of such a card. Sheila (my sister) had written to the barracks and told them about Victoria, asking if they could possibly send her a get well card, explaining that she loved horses and had, with Joanna, sent Sefton a card when he had been injured. But we had never imagined that she might be invited to the barracks to see him. We all looked forward eagerly to hearing when it would be. Sheila could never have foreseen what she had put in motion when she wrote that first letter to the Household Cavalry and just how much it would come to mean, to Victoria especially.

We had been told by the Physiotherapist at Roehampton that swimming would be excellent for Victoria. It would help strengthen all the muscles needed to help her walk with the artificial leg. She adored swimming anyway. Jill, her favourite nurse, who happened to live in the same village, had suggested before we left the hospital that when she next had a day off she would love to come to the pool with us. I was pleased, as we set out for the pool a few days after the homecoming, that Jill had offered to come. I was a little apprehensive about it. How would Victoria get on? Would it be the beginning of resentment and frustration at not being able to do things as she had done before? As we lowered ourselves into the water and helped Victoria in, I found myself wondering just how she would cope. I should have realised. Jill and I were left standing in the shallow end of the pool, like a couple of lemons staring after my daughter! She was swimming towards the deep end as if nothing at all had happened. She could swim as well as ever, my fears had been completely dispelled and proved groundless. Here was something she was able to do as well as she had before the amputation. Even she was excited. She told us afterwards that she was unsure beforehand that she would still be able to swim, but once in the pool she was on equal terms with the other children and could swim as well as most and better than some. Consequently we made several visits to the pool during the following weeks. Victoria never tired of it and we always had a battle getting her out before she turned blue with the cold. No-one was ever going to call her handicapped. I think that was the one thing she feared and her confidence increased daily. She seemed to have an inner strength, unusual in one so young.

About a week before the long awaited move into our new house, the anticipated letter from the barracks duly arrived. It was addressed to Victoria. She opened it excitedly, having seen the crest on the back of the envelope. It was from Captain Harry Scott, the Adjutant to the Household Cavalry Regiment, and was a formal invitation for us to visit the barracks on either the tenth or eleventh of November. The reply was sent by return of post, to say that we would love to come on the tenth, as she was going to Roehampton on the eleventh. It was her most important appointment so far, for she was at last to get her 'NEW LEG'.

During the next few days we were all kept more than busy with the big move and all that it involved, the packing and sorting out, the curtains to be made and altered. Surprisingly Victoria even wanted to come with me when I went into the town to buy some more curtain material and was quite helpful in choosing from the vast array we were confronted with. I had thought she might find it rather exhausting, wandering between the different shops, but she seemed thoroughly to enjoy it. However, the outing disturbed me slightly. It was the way people stared at her when they saw the crutches. Their stares became even more curious when they saw that she only had one leg. Naturally, at home in our own little parade of shops everyone knew her and what she had been through. I hadn't bargained for this. It didn't seem to bother Victoria in the least, therefore, I suppose, it shouldn't have bothered me. But it did. I suppose it is something to do with a mother's natural protective instinct towards her offspring. It really got to me, especially when people screwed their heads round to get a better look, even to the extent of one or two of them practically falling over themselves in the process. But then, had I not been guilty in the past, before any of this had happened to us, of perhaps looking too long at someone in a wheelchair? Victoria anyway had enjoyed her day out and had spent ages in her favourite shop, buying several bits and pieces that I knew Alan would think of as rubbish. But it was her own money, given to her by relatives and friends when they had visited her in hospital.

It was only afterwards, as we travelled home in the car, that I began to wish I had taken a little more notice of what she had been buying.

'Would you like a sweet, Mummy?' she asked. 'They're peppermint ones.'

'Mm, yes please,' I replied innocently. 'Could you take the wrapper off for me?'

She handed me the sweet which I quickly put into my mouth as we were approaching a junction. Shortly afterwards the early pleasant peppermint flavour changed to the most foul taste it has ever been my misfortune to sample; one that I can only describe as a cross between very hot pepper and ground chilli powder, with a bit of mustard thrown in for good measure.

I could hardly speak. 'Ugh! What on earth is it?'

Victoria of course was convulsed with laughter in the back seat, hardly able to control herself, but she managed to explain, as if I didn't know, that they were 'joke sweets'. Some joke, I thought! I had to promise that I would not mention them to either Alan or Joanna as she was hoping to catch them out too.

'I can't wait to see Jo's face,' she said with glee. Neither could I. She was what one might describe as being rather partial to sweets. This brand, however, I felt might just prove to be the exception. Mine had been hastily thrown out of the car window. I just hoped that some poor unsuspecting dog did not chance to find it.

Joanna didn't quite see the joke, but it did put her off sweets for, well, at least twenty-four hours. Alan wasn't quite so easily fooled but he pretended he had been caught out too, so as not to spoil the fun.

# CHAPTER
## 8

At last we were in our new home. It was wonderful after the past few months of cramped living to have so much space all to ourselves. After the problem of too much furniture in a small house, we now felt that what we had was not going to make much impression.

Victoria was as excited as any of us by the move, especially as two friends, David and Fiona, who had helped us out in the pub we had had in Cumbria two years previously, came to stay and helped with the move. As usual when the Harts move house, it was done in a hired van. I've always said that if I was ever stuck for a job, I'm sure Pickfords would take me on.

We had not seen David and Fiona for some months and they felt a little apprehensive, as did many people, about meeting Victoria again, fearing that she must in some way be affected by what she had been through, even though we had tried to reassure them over the telephone that this was not the case. They were therefore quite unprepared for the live wire who greeted them on their arrival, and who also did a fair share of all the packing and tidying up, never complaining, other than when she felt that Joanna was not pulling her weight when it came to sorting out the mess in their bedroom. That was nothing new; she was always very good at making a mess, but hopeless about clearing up after she had finished anything, with the excuse it hadn't been her fault. Well, things were going to be different now; Joanna might be in for rather a shock, for they now had a bedroom each. She would not be able to blame anyone else for any untidyness in her room.

We all had great fun that weekend, and to Victoria's great delight she discovered that Fiona didn't like spiders. On a shopping trip with Alan and David she persuaded them to buy a large, black and very hairy fake spider. This she proceeded to put into Fiona's bed that night. The screams issuing forth later were enough to prove that her little joke had gone as planned. Fiona and David later left for their homeward journey, amazed at Victoria's obvious confidence and happiness, despite all she had been through.

The first Thursday in November brought Victoria's visit to the clinic, the first of the three-monthly check-ups to make sure that the cancer had not spread and that her lungs in particular were not affected. The clinic was run by Mr Steel and the Consultant Radiologist (cancer specialist) at the hospital. Knowing that there was a risk of the cancer spreading, especially within the next five years, was something that was never very far from our thoughts. Having said that, it would be wrong to give the impression that this thought was constantly in our minds. It wasn't. Taking our cue from Victoria herself, we learnt to play each day as it came and not to worry about what might happen. All that could be done thus far had been done. She too knew that the risk was there.

So it was that we all experienced a certain amount of

apprehension and nervousness as we made our way to the X-ray department, after checking in at the desk. The chest X-ray would be a regular feature of these visits and would reveal whether or not the thing we dreaded most had been controlled: that the cancer had not spread.

Sitting in the consulting room afterwards, we had a desultory conversation as we waited anxiously for the Consultants to come back and tell us, we prayed, that all was well. The door opened and we looked towards it expectantly. Mr Steel and his colleague, a very jovial man, who was always wisecracking with Victoria, entered the small room, which suddenly began to feel claustrophobic.

'Well, Victoria, we've just seen some lovely pictures of your chest, and they all look very good,' said Mr Steel. 'When do you get your leg from Roehampton?'

'Next week,' she answered. 'And guess what, I had a card from Sefton, the horse that was injured by a bomb, and we're going to see him next week too, at the barracks in Knightsbridge.'

I hardly listened to the rest of what was said. Our relief on hearing his words was almost indescribable. I could sense the release of tension all round, followed by an almost euphoric sense of gaiety. We would now try to put it behind us, for three months at least, until the next visit at the beginning of February.

The impending outing to see Sefton had been generating excitement for some weeks. This was heightened the day before by the fact that Alan had been in touch with our local Sussex newspaper, who said they would be delighted to cover the event in their edition of the following week. I managed to persuade Victoria to come to the hairdressers. She was in the process of growing her hair long and had defied all attempts so far at least to have it trimmed. She agreed this time, but I felt rather sorry for the poor girl whose task the trim was, for Victoria never once took her eyes off her, making certain that only the smallest amount was cut off.

We arrived home to find Alan on the telephone in the hall, so crept past him quietly, wondering who it was. As Victoria said, he had his 'telephone voice' on. When he finished the conversation he came through to announce to us excitedly that he had been speaking to the editor of a well-known national daily newspaper. They wanted to do a story about Victoria's meeting with Sefton, having heard about it from our own local paper. Apparently several of the national papers had been in touch, and one of them was even sending a photographer down that very afternoon, so that they could have 'before' and 'after' photographs in the article. Victoria seemed the least concerned by all this fuss, as she put it. Although she always looked forward to seeing the results in the press, she never at any time revelled in all the attendant publicity, finding it instead rather incomprehensible that she should warrant such attention in the first place. This again underlined her attitude to the whole issue. She could still do the things that she wanted to do. If she had not had her leg amputated she might have died. No-one knew that better than Alan and I, and life was for living not for looking back and thinking what might have been. As several of our friends had told us, her manner had a very humbling effect on all of them, making them feel guilty of even thinking about their minor aches and pains, let alone talking about them out loud. We knew only too well how they felt.

The photographer eventually arrived, after losing his

way twice in the surrounding country lanes. He spent ages taking shots both inside the house and out, some of Victoria with our dog Heather, some on her own and some with Alan and me. Of course when it came down to it, there was only the smallest picture in the paper the next day.

We had stopped at our local newsagents on our way up to London to see if anything had resulted from the photographer's visit. We saw the small picture of Victoria and a few paragraphs telling how the forthcoming meeting with Sefton had come about. We explained to the newsagent what was going on and he promised to look through all the papers the following day when they came in and to keep aside any that had covered the story.

On our arrival at the barracks at the appointed time, we were faintly surprised and rather amused to see that some members of the press had beaten us to it and were waiting with cameras primed for our arrival. We were greeted by Captain Harry Scott, the Adjutant of the Household Cavalry, who had arranged for the visit to take place. At the time of our arrival, the Guard was in the process of being inspected prior to taking up their duties at Horse Guards. As Her Majesty The Queen was in residence in London, the Royal Standard would be carried, making the occasion even more significant for us. We watched from some steps as the ritual of the inspection continued, then the salute was taken and the troop went on their way. It was a marvellous sight indeed, enhanced by the fact, as we were later to be told, that this was an event that had taken place continuously for the last two hundred years despite two world wars and the terrorist bombing.

Once the Guard had left, all the attention turned to

Victoria. She had become a little nervous on seeing all the cameras when we approached. Captain Scott suggested wisely that when Sefton was brought out it would be a good idea to let the press get their shots over with first and then we could enjoy a more leisurely look round the rest of the barracks, in peace. No-one was more relieved by his words than Victoria, who had dreaded being trailed by photographers at every turn.

Sefton was duly led out by the man who rode him on that fateful July day, Trooper Pederson. He had also been injured in the cowardly attack but had thankfully recovered. Sefton looked magnificent. We would not have guessed how severely he had been injured only four months before. I would not like to calculate just how many rolls of film the various photographers used that day, but I suppose they use similar amounts covering all newsworthy stories. After about ten minutes a halt was called, but not before one bright spark had suggested placing a well known brand of mint just inside Victoria's ear, to see if Sefton would retrieve it. I was relieved that Captain Scott felt that enough was enough. I couldn't have agreed more and cannot repeat what Victoria said about the incident afterwards.

We were then introduced to Squadron Corporal-Major Mike Brown of the Blues and Royals, Sefton's regiment. The Household Cavalry consists of squadrons of two regiments—the Blues and Royals and the Life Guards. Corporal-Major Brown was marvellous, making us feel most welcome and explaining everything to us as he showed us round. He was especially good with Victoria, treating her completely normally, which was exactly what she wished from everyone. Thus he gained her instant respect and confidence. She was always slightly suspicious of those who gave any overt display of sympathy or treated her differently in any way. Her wish was to lead a completely normal life.

The whole day was an unforgettable experience for us all, as there was so much that was new to see; all the beautiful uniforms, many of which we had previously seen only on television as they are kept for state occasions, with their gold thread embroidery that made them extremely heavy. The highly polished helmets weighed even more as the girls discovered when they were invited to try one on. We all felt it would be quite an exhausting experience to have to wear the full regalia on horseback for even a few hours; most state occasions last considerably longer.

We toured the saddlery and the tailors' department, and of course we couldn't ignore the forge. Here all the horses are shod. The shoes are much larger than normal, due to all the hard work put in on the London streets.

One of the highlights for the girls on reaching the stables was seeing the two enormous drum horses, Caractacus and Coriolanus. They have to be big to carry the huge silver kettledrums. The girls were asked if they would like to sit on the back of one of them. Caractacus was chosen and Corporal-Major Brown lifted each of them in turn onto the great horse's back. They said afterwards that it was rather frightening looking down on us all from such a great height. I certainly didn't envy them their experience.

We continued on our way to see the room where all the harnesses are stored and the supplies of hay and fodder, and of course the stables themselves. It was hard to remember whilst being shown round that we were still in the heart of Knightsbridge, because it was like a completely self-contained little town of its own.

To round off our tour, we were taken to the indoor riding school. There we saw not only horses new to the Household Cavalry being put through their paces, but riders too, some there for their first ceremonial duties and others on a refresher course.

Before we left, Corporal-Major Brown took us for coffee in the NCO's Mess, where Captain Scott came to say goodbye. They had a surprise for Victoria first, and her happiness was complete when they presented her with a large framed replica of the Regiment's insignia, which had been made by one of the troopers. She was really quite overcome by their kindness and thanked them shyly, saying that as soon as she returned home it would have pride of place on her bedroom wall.

Corporal-Major Brown escorted us to the gate. We felt that we could not thank him or Captain Scott enough for the wonderful day we had all enjoyed. As we said goodbye, he knelt down to kiss Victoria, and knowing she was to collect her artificial leg the following day, said to her, 'I'm going to make a bargain with you, all right?'

She nodded silently, a slightly puzzled look on her face, wondering, as we were, what was coming next.

'When you've got your new leg and you can walk without sticks or crutches, will you promise to write and tell me?'

'Yes, I will,' she replied, still slightly puzzled.

'Well, when you do, I'll ask your Mum and Dad if they can bring you back to see us again, and Sefton of course. You won't forget, will you?'

'Oh no, of course I won't,' she gasped with delight. 'Thank you very much.'

Victoria was thrilled by this marvellous gesture and so

were we. He was a professional soldier, and in this capacity he must have seen many injuries and worse while serving with the Army in Northern Ireland and the recent Falklands conflict for example. But something about Victoria had touched him deeply despite this. It meant so much to her. Did he realise how much? None of us could quite know at that stage.

Next day several of the national newspapers carried reports and some lovely pictures of Victoria with Sefton. We collected them eagerly on our way to Roehampton. The newsagent, being almost as excited as we were, had already looked through them all and put to one side copies of all those which carried the story.

The power of the press was again evident when we arrived at Roehampton. All the staff had seen the papers and of course wanted to know all about the visit. A more amusing incident occurred when we were in the waiting room. I could see that several people were reading one of the newspapers that carried a large picture of the previous day's events. Several of them had looked up from scanning the pages, seen Victoria, and quickly looked back to the paper, then back to Victoria again, just to make sure this was the same little girl. She found it highly amusing and great fun, but she said she was glad she was not a member of the Royal Family or a pop star.

We did not have too long to wait before John, who was making Victoria's leg, came to take us through to the fitting room. She could not wait to get there, knowing that at last she would have her new leg. She shot off after John, so missing the arrival of Sally, the Physiotherapist who worked on some of Mr Steel's cases. Sally had wanted to come today, not least because the design of the leg was so new and she had not seen one before. The main reason, however, was that as Victoria would only have one week's walking training with the Physiotherapists at Roehampton, she might well need a little extra help from Sally once she was home. Sally would have to see how they dealt with the situation and have the workings of the leg explained. We all hurried down the corridor after Victoria.

Victoria was pleased to see Sally again, although her mind was really on one thing only — THE LEG. When John duly arrived with it in his arms, it turned out to be unlike anything Sally had ever seen before and I can only describe it as amazing. Once Victoria had put it on, it appeared even more so. It was shaped so much like her own that I doubt anyone who was not a party to the truth would ever have guessed.

She took several steps down the length of the room, which was furnished with a set of parallel bars for this purpose, and managed with what seemed to us supreme competence. She had been warned that it might take some time before she was able to master the art of walking unaided and that she would have to be patient. Nothing daunted, Victoria was just planning to get on with what she knew she must. She was determined to succeed in as short a time as possible, even though she knew it meant a lot of hard work. Later, during her walking training, she did admit to feeling rather tired in the evenings, due to the weight of the leg and, as Alan said, the fact that she would rarely take a rest. She never complained about it. All she could think of was the time when she would be able to return to school and to a normal life. This, I'm sure, spurred her on to the goal she had set herself.

After this final fitting, however, there were one or two

minor adjustments to be made to the leg before we could leave for home, but these did not take long and gave us the time we needed to make arrangements for Victoria to attend the walking school the following week. It had at first been thought that she would need to stay in the hospital at Roehampton for that week and that I would stay with her, as she had asked. This was something that neither Victoria nor I particularly relished. Having seen her use the leg, the Physiotherapists now felt that she was going to learn much faster than anyone had anticipated. As we lived only about an hour's car journey away, they wondered if we could bring her up daily instead. This arrangement suited us all, naturally, and most especially Victoria. We thought that it would be best if Alan was the one to bring her up and she herself was quite agreeable to this. I don't think either of them trusted my driving in all that traffic! But I would be able to take Joanna to school, making up to her in some part for all the hours I had missed with her over the past few weeks.

As we left through the glass doors of the limb-fitting centre, Alan rushed off ahead. I had an idea of what he was up to, but said nothing. As we three emerged into the chill Autumn sunshine he was there, camera in hand, ready to capture Victoria's first steps forever on cine film, just as he had done on her first birthday. Why I should have thought of that, at that precise moment, is hard to explain, but perhaps it was just the fact that the camera itself had been bought with Green Shield stamps especially for that occasion, just over ten years ago. I was brought out of my reverie by Victoria asking me to look at her legs. Did I notice anything rather odd? Oh Lord! I had forgotten to bring a spare sock. I had got used to putting out only one. But I had promised myself that today of all days I must remember, and I hadn't. It did look rather strange to see her now, with two legs—and only one sock. I could have kicked myself. It was made worse by the fact that we had planned to stop on the way home for something to eat. What were we going to do? As luck would have it, we managed to find a small drapers shop on the way and were able to buy a pair, much to Victoria's relief.

She was still, of course, using her crutches in conjunction with the artificial leg, and would be given a pair of sticks when she went up next week for her walking training. As we went into the restaurant we had chosen, a waitress came towards us to show us to a free table. She glanced at Victoria's legs and then asked, 'What have you been up to then? Broken your ankle?'

Victoria could hardly control her giggles as she replied, 'No, I haven't broken it.'

None of us knew quite what to say, so it was just glossed over as we were shown to a table. It struck all of us that no-one had had to ask before. What was wrong had been plain for all to see. Victoria was as pleased as punch to think that her new leg looked real enough for people to wonder only if she had hurt herself because of the crutches. It reminded me of an incident at the local supermarket a few days earlier. Victoria had come with me to do the weekly shopping. At the check-out queue, the poor assistant had seen Victoria's crutches from her seat at the till and being rather a pleasant and friendly girl had said as she leaned over the counter towards Victoria, 'What have you been up to then?'

I felt sorry for her when she eventually leaned over far enough to see the truth. Poor girl, she was so apologetic. It hadn't bothered Victoria at all and she too expressed how sorry she felt for the assistant. For weeks afterwards I wanted to go back and reassure her that it was all right, but of course I never did and it is something I still regret to this day.

Before finally going home that day, we naturally called in on Alan's parents to show them this marvellous leg they had heard so much about. Of course, they were as amazed as we had been by its appearance. We were invited to stay for tea, but for some mysterious reason Victoria seemed more anxious than usual to get home. Anyway, as we explained, we were all feeling rather tired after the excitement of the last two days, so we declined. I did wonder why Victoria had been so adamant about getting home. I didn't have to wait long before I found out.

'Can I have my bicycle out of the shed when we get home please, Daddy?'

Stunned silence, as we digested thoroughly what she had said, now realising the need to rush home. She couldn't, I thought. How on earth would she be able to ride her bike?

'But it will soon be dark,' I prevaricated. 'Why don't you wait until the morning?'

But she was not to be dissuaded, and as soon as we were out of the car Alan went round to the shed to get her bike, Joanna following closely on his heels. She was certainly not going to be left out of this. Being younger than her sister, it had always been she who had been left behind when cycling or running. I think she felt that she would perhaps at last be able to do something a little better than Victoria.

'Listen, Victoria,' I said to her, 'you mustn't be too upset if you can't ride it straight away. It might take a bit

Joanna pushing Victoria in the go-cart she helped to make

Who said I can't climb trees?

of practice.' Her look said, 'Mum's fussing again.' I tried not to, but it was mighty difficult at times like this. It wasn't for myself that I was worrying, I just didn't want her to be too upset by the frustration of not being able to do something which before the amputation she had been very adept at. 'I'll be all right, don't worry, Mummy, but I want to do it.'

Alan and Joanna rounded the corner of the house with the bicycles. Alan helped Victoria onto the saddle and then held onto the back of it as she went up and down the drive a couple of times. Joanna had been off like a shot, feeling as I had thought she might. Talk about one-upmanship! It was not to last for long.

'Let go now, Daddy,' came Victoria's voice, 'I can do it on my own now.'

Alan looked over to where I was standing with an expression that said, What else can I do? He looked back towards Victoria. 'Are you sure? You might wobble off.'

Would she be able to balance on her own?

'Go on, Daddy, let go. I'll be all right.'

He did as he was bid. I could hardly bear to watch, but, of course I did. Miraculously she seemed completely competent and well able to ride the bicycle on her own. It seemed that the weight of the artificial limb was enough to force down the left hand pedal enough to raise the right hand pedal high enough for her to push it down again with the force of her own leg. In fact in only a matter of weeks she was able to ride without the artificial limb at all, just using her one leg. We could hardly believe the evidence of our own eyes and yet there she was, full of confidence. She would have stayed out all night if we had let her. The expression on her face, when they did come inside, said it all. She was thrilled that she had been able to manage it, on her own too.

'I didn't really think I'd be able to do it, and you didn't think I would either, did you?' she exclaimed, absolutely glowing. I had to admit that I had been doubtful. Mr Steel's words came back to me, when he told her that if she really wanted to do something, she would do it. I realised how right he was. Who was I to tell her she could or could not do something? It was up to her to do whatever she felt she could. Alan and I realised then that she would have a go at almost anything.

# CHAPTER
## 9
---

The following week, as planned, Alan drove Victoria up to Roehampton every day, to the walking school. They left just before eight o'clock and spent most of the day there.

She started off by just walking backwards and forwards between the parallel bars, from which she progressed to walking on her own, with the aid of the two sticks she had been given. Unbelievably, they were made from Brussels sprout stalks, as she told us later, after having asked us to try and guess what they were. None of us guessed correctly.

She was soon walking up and down the ramps and steps, and by the end of the week could manage with only one stick for support, so it looked as though Sally's help would not be necessary the following week. Victoria soon became a familiar sight in the hospital grounds as she accompanied her helper, Mary, on various errands to different departments.

Most of the other amputees attending the school at that time were generally considerably older than Victoria, and she would amuse us in the evenings with stories of their lack of eagerness to experiment with their newly acquired limbs. We had to explain that being much older than her, they did not share her enthusiasm and found it all rather trying and hard. But I'm afraid she found it very difficult to understand why anyone would not want to learn to walk again.

She had, however, met one younger person on her first day there, an Egyptian girl in her early twenties who had lost her leg in a car accident. She had been fitted with the same type of limb as Victoria. Victoria and Alan were greatly impressed that when she had walked out of the hospital to return to Egypt, she was only using one stick. No-one would have guessed she had an artificial leg. Meeting her so early in the week had certainly boosted Victoria's confidence and her will to do at least as well, if not better. She did indeed do much better than anyone could have predicted, and on her last day at the school was photographed for promotional purposes, wearing the leg. As it was so new and she had learnt to cope with it so quickly, it was causing much interest. She had already given a demonstration to an Under-Secretary from the Ministry of Health and Social Security, and had another scheduled in a few months' time for a delegation from Japan. It was nice to think that we could teach them something at last!

It seemed impossible that only ten weeks had passed since the operation had taken place and just twelve weeks since we had first heard what had been such devastating news. Now here Victoria was walking again, making sure that the loss of her leg would never prove to her to be a disability. She had undergone countless tests, scans and X-rays, which to most adults would have been irksome, to say the least. Yet she had come through it all with an amazing courage and cheerfulness that had put us to shame. We looked forward to the future with new hope and the certainty that life would return to a more routine footing, the start of which was the long and eagerly awaited return to school.

The great day arrived. Victoria must have been awake for hours: she was already dressed in her school uniform when I went along to their rooms to tell them that it was time to get up. She was busily packing her bag with all the usual accoutrements associated with school life.

'Did you get me a new gym skirt and leotard and tights, Mum?' she asked. 'Because Joanna had my others, they were too small for me.'

I was stopped in my tracks by her inquiry, having been on my way to rouse Joanna. It had never occurred to me that she would even want to attempt gym and games. I had assumed, wrongly, as it was turning out, that she would give these lessons a miss feeling perhaps embarrassed in front of the other girls. I really should have learnt by now, especially after the episode of the bicycle. But what about the other girls? What would their reactions be, seeing Victoria with only one leg? She wouldn't be able to take part wearing the artificial leg, it was much too heavy. Children could be so cruel without meaning to be. But who was I to worry if Victoria was so unconcerned? I certainly couldn't give an outright 'no'.

'Well, you don't have gym or anything today,' I said gaily, 'so I'll pop into town while you're at school and buy the things you'll need, OK?'

That question settled, I left Victoria to finish her packing as I continued on my way into Joanna's room to see if I could wake her; not an easy task, I might add, as she was like a little dormouse and hated to leave her cosy 'nest' to get dressed for school. It was a different matter at the weekends. Then, when everyone else wanted a little longer in bed, she would be awake at the crack of dawn, pestering us all to get up. However, on this particular day she seemed as excited by the prospect of her sister's return to school as any of us and dressed without much complaint. I think she felt she might be able to help Victoria a bit at school, if needed. Funnily enough, she was the only person Victoria would allow to do the occasional little thing to help her, and it made her feel all the more grown-up. If anyone else offered assistance it was a different matter. Victoria valued her independence too much to want to rely on others.

Once breakfast was over and it was time to leave, there was the usual last minute scramble for hats and coats. I could never understand how this always happened, even when we seemed to arrive downstairs with ample time before we had to leave. Extra time was needed to allow Victoria to put her leg on, but at last we were in the car and on our way.

'Are you a bit nervous?' I asked Victoria, thinking she seemed rather quieter than usual.

'Oh no, I'm just excited. I can't wait to see all my friends again.' She sounded surprised. Was I fussing again? I really would have to stop.

She had asked me to walk down to her classroom with her. It was situated several hundred yards from the car park and she could not carry her bag and cope with the sticks at the same time. Although she could now manage without any aids for walking, we had been told that when she was anywhere with a lot of people it would be advisable to have the sticks for support, in case she was jostled or pushed accidentally. The wisdom of this decision soon became apparent as the girls began rushing up to her excitedly, welcoming her back to school. They were all dying to hear about her visit to Sefton. I felt so much happier about her return to school, which had naturally worried me, when I saw the other girls' easy acceptance of her. They were trying so hard not to look at her legs and there were no comments whatsoever.

Victoria thoroughly enjoyed being back at school at last and it didn't take long before she gave her classmates a full demonstration of THE LEG — how it was made and how it worked. I felt it was marvellous that she had the confidence to be able to do this; the others must have felt rather curious about it and in this way all their questions were out of the way right at the beginning. They were quite happy that their curiosity had been satisfied and Victoria was glad that they knew what it was all about.

There were one or two minor problems to be sorted out but nothing to do with the way she behaved or managed to cope with things. No, the first was something I should really have thought about beforehand. The artificial leg, because of its construction, the way it fitted round her hips like a fibreglass corset, made sitting on a hard wooden school chair for any length of time extremely uncomfortable. This was soon rectified by buying a thick piece of foam rubber for the chair of the type used for upholstery. After this, if it still became uncomfortable she would, without any fuss and quite naturally, just rise from her seat and remove her leg at the back of the classroom, leaving it there against the wall for a while. People soon became quite used to seeing it and no comments were ever made to me about it.

The other slight problem had proved rather more upsetting for Victoria and concerned the fact that during playtime, when it was usual for all the children to go outside to the playground if the weather was fine, she had been made to stay in the classroom, choosing a friend to stay in with her. Despite none of them being very keen to stay inside anyway, she herself had been eager to go out with the others. It was one of the things about school which she had been looking forward to. I could understand the reasons behind it. The staff must have been worried in case she fell and injured herself. With all the other children around it was of course a possibility. But it was something she had to be allowed to do. She didn't want to be made to feel unlike the others. Nobody must make her feel that she was different; she knew her limitations. As I was explaining this to her form teacher, I felt that now would be a good time to tell her that Victoria would be taking part in all games and gymnastic classes. There were a few moments of shocked silence, as I had guessed there might be after the playground incident, before she answered, albeit rather uncertainly, 'Yes, of course . . .'

By the end of her first week at school, the staff were beginning to realise, as we had had to do, that there was no stopping her. She was so determined to do everything the other girls did and it would have been extremely unfair to have forbidden any of the activities she wished to take part in.

We had encountered slight barriers even before her return to school, before the operation, with people constantly telling us what she wouldn't be able to do. One official in particular, who had come to see us before the operation, had made everything seem insurmountable. I was told that after the operation, before we could take her swimming, we should contact the staff at the pool, so that Victoria could go to special sessions for the disabled. Of course I did no such thing and there was never any problem. It would have gone down like a ton of bricks with Victoria, had she known of the suggestion. There had been endless queries about how many steps she would have to negotiate at school? How far did she have to walk from her classroom to the dining room? Was the school insured for her to take part in all its activities? I suppose these basically well-meaning people were only doing their jobs, but we did find it all rather disheartening, as if they wanted to stop her from doing things, rather than give encouragement. They certainly didn't know Victoria very well.

All of the staff at the school and the pupils themselves were marvellous and never—after the minor incidents of the first days had been cleared up—treated her in any way differently from anyone else. That was exactly the way she wanted it to be. She neither expected nor received any special privileges and she would have hated things to be otherwise.

Victoria soon settled back into the routine of school life and became again just one of the girls. One of her greatest joys was seeing her best friend Emma again, and they resumed their visits to each other's houses for tea after school. After one such visit to Emma's home I learned to my astonishment that they had played at being Tarzan, swinging from a rope in a tree! My amazement was nothing compared with that of Emma's mother, who couldn't believe how naturally Victoria behaved, as if nothing at all had happened.

Homework was the only thing Victoria complained about. It had always seemed to her a bit of a chore. There were usually much more interesting things to be done, but she always managed to get it finished, although sometimes not until the following morning just before leaving for school.

She was delighted when the school started rehearsals for the Nativity play at the end of November, and that she would be in it. Both she and Joanna amongst several others were to be shepherds. I willingly agreed to see to their costumes, using a couple of Alan's old shirts and the inevitable tea towels and dressing gown cords that seem to turn up in most Nativity plays.

Netball, too, was being played during this term, weather permitting. Victoria had always enjoyed net-ball, and saw no reason why this should change, although, not surprisingly, she now found it considerably more tiring than before, having only one leg to hop around on. It would have been impossible for her to have worn the artificial leg for any sport. Apart from its weight, there was the danger of injury to herself and possibly to others. There was also the fact that the limb might be damaged in some way, and as the spare one was not yet ready that would have meant her being without the leg at all while it was being repaired. However, nothing deterred her and despite the exhaustion she was still determined to take part. The teacher suggested that she should take short rests during the game, and had a chair brought out for her for this purpose. This was the only concession that Victoria ever allowed and the only one in the circumstances that was entirely necessary, although Victoria hated it and was pleased when after a few weeks she was able to manage without resting.

Her other great love was gymnastics, her great regret about all that had happened being that she felt sure she would not now be asked to join the school gymnastic club, which she had been on the verge of joining prior to the operation. However, a few days after her return, I chanced to bump into her gym mistress, on my way down to Victoria's classroom at the end of the day. Mrs Barnes asked me how things were going and said that Victoria seemed to be coping extremely well with school life.

'I've been meaning to ask Victoria if she would like to join the school gym club? She really is doing remarkably well in class.'

'She would be absolutely thrilled,' I replied, rather stunned, as I had been wondering how I would be able to console Victoria when she realised that she probably would not get into the club.

'She was saying only the other day that she didn't think she stood a chance of joining now.' Then, as the thought crossed my mind as I was sure it would Victoria's, 'She wouldn't want to think that she has only been asked because of what has happened?'

'Oh no, of course not. I'd have asked her anyway at the beginning of term, if she had been here,' she answered, knowing exactly what I had meant.

'You know, it's hard to believe, seeing her in class, that there is anything wrong. She just carries on without any fuss and tries everything that the others do. It's quite incredible and she's always got such a happy smile on her face. She looks so full of joy, she makes one feel quite inadequate.'

I knew exactly what she meant and I felt so proud of Victoria. We were beginning to think that she did indeed have extraordinary courage. But then of course we were her parents and biased in our opinions. It was all the more special when one hears such comments from others, particularly those outside the family circle and unconnected with us except in a casual way.

Life at last seemed to have returned to its former

routine and normality, with the girls both back at school and Alan able to return to working full-time for his father. For myself, I found it rather hard to go back to the household chores that made up my day, having been needed so much over the last few weeks. It was not easy to settle down and I had more time on my hands to worry. But how could I let things get me down with Victoria around? It was impossible. Anyway, Christmas was ahead, so I was kept pretty busy with all the preparations for it. I was determined that this year would be one of the happiest we had ever had, after all we had been through. I felt that we all deserved that much. We had intended to go for a holiday abroad once things returned to normal, but now that the house was at last completed and furnished more or less to our satisfaction, we could not afford a holiday as well. Perhaps next year?

We did indeed have a wonderful Christmas and it holds many happy memories for us all. I expect we all ate too much and did little to exert ourselves physically during the holiday period. But after the traumas of the previous months, it was just what we needed. My parents and my sister Sheila were able to come and stay with us and we saw a few friends including, happily, Jill, Victoria's favourite nurse, and her husband Neil. It was a family time when we enjoyed playing games with the girls and took pleasure in just being together. I feel that it was special in some way. I suppose everyone thinks that way with hindsight. But perhaps hindsight is necessary to make us see things in that light.

The holidays seemed to pass with alarming speed. Fortunately the weather had been fairly mild, allowing the girls to play in the garden quite a bit. Garden is perhaps too grand a word to describe the land surrounding our house at that time. It still resembled a builders' yard, and having heavy clay soil it would have to wait until the early Spring before we were able to do anything with it. This, however, did not seem to bother either Victoria or Joanna, who were able to ride their bikes around and climb one of the old apple trees. And, yes, Victoria was the first one up the tree! It was no good my telling her to be careful. Indeed, I had learnt my lesson on that score. I received a blank stare when I suggested that care should be taken, as if to remind me that yet again I was being over fussy. I would just have to learn to bite my tongue in future.

That Victoria was willing to try anything was brought home to us even more vividly one Sunday near the end of the holidays. As it was such a lovely afternoon we decided to go for a walk after lunch. The girls said they wanted to go through the woods next to the house, despite the fact that the paths were slightly rutted, which wouldn't make the going very easy for Victoria. My meek suggestion that Alan might have to carry her over some places was dismissed impatiently.

'Oh, don't be silly, Mummy. I can do it. Anyway, I'll have to start practising for the sponsored walk at school. It's not long until May.'

Good grief, she didn't think she'd be able to do that this year? But I knew she did. It had been a statement; she wasn't asking if she could. She was telling us that she was going to take part and woe betide anyone who tried to stop her. What would she come up with next? I would not have been entirely surprised if she had suggested a course in mountaineering. It was obvious now that she was going to let nothing defeat her, despite what anyone else thought.

# CHAPTER
## 10

Once the holidays were over the date for Victoria's second checkup at the clinic, the first Thursday in February, seemed to come upon us with alarming speed. The thought of what it might reveal had been on our minds for several days before, although we tried not to dwell on it too much.

A telephone call from Mr Steel a couple of days before we were due to see him went some way towards helping us to turn our thoughts elsewhere. He had called to say that unhappily he had just had to perform the very same operation, for the same reason, on another little girl. As she was only four years old, it was proving particularly worrying for all concerned. Knowing that we would be bringing Victoria into the clinic on Thursday, he wondered if we would mind going to see her and her parents at the other hospital afterwards. He felt sure that if they could see how well Victoria was doing it would give them a lot of encouragement. I said that we would be only too pleased to help in any way we could. I knew exactly how her parents must be feeling.

Victoria was full of compassion for four-year-old Demelza Spruce and looked forward to meeting her. 'It must be much worse for her, because she's so much younger. I'll be able to show her what my leg is like. She'll be able to have one too, won't she?'

I said I thought it was highly probable. I couldn't help thinking how strange it was, with a disease as rare as Osteogenic Sarcoma, that Mr Steel should have two cases in the space of just six months. I only hoped that we would be able to be of some support to this other family.

Victoria was continuing to do well and had more or less made up at school the ground she had lost through her protracted absence the previous term. Her only regret was that Emma had left to go to another school. Victoria still had plenty of other friends, but Emma had been her special friend. They still kept in touch, and I found their phone calls to each other rather amusing. They were accompanied by a mixture of giggling and long silences, during which neither of them seemed to know what to say. After all that, there would be another call the following day. No wonder they ran out of conversation! They managed to see each other too, exchanging visits at weekends. On one such visit to our house they were playing about with a cassette recorder, pretending they were doing a radio show. I must say the end result was quite good: the usual 'knock knock' jokes and the like, but what had really given it the 'professional' touch was that Victoria had had the idea of shaking a tin of marbles, to give the effect of audience applause. It certainly did just that. It took us ages to puzzle out where they had found a real audience, until we were let in on the secret.

Thursday arrived all too quickly. We reached the clinic in good time for Victoria's appointment and were duly sent down for the regular chest X-ray, after her weight had been checked. They were amazed to see that she had gained rather a lot since her last visit, until we realised that the previous checkup had taken place before she had her artificial leg. So she had to remove it in order that her weight could be gauged correctly. I think, at first, they must have wondered what I was feeding her on.

When the Consultants came into the room where we were waiting, it was, as it had been the last time, difficult to discern anything from either their expressions or their manner, especially as the conversation was mainly about her visit to see Sefton. Mr Steel, of course, was very interested in her limb. He had not seen her since she had been fitted with it. In fact he, and everyone else, had not seen this kind before. He told her that he had heard from others that she had a 'bionic' leg and he was most impressed by it.

As they were leaving the consulting room, I realised that nothing had been said of the chest X-ray. Should I ask? They would surely have told us if something had been wrong?

Then the Radiologist turned to Mr Steel, and said quite casually, 'I think it's about time she had another scan, don't you?'

'Yes, I should think so. You don't mind, do you Victoria?' She shook her head. 'Will next week some-time be all right?' I said that would be fine, but why, I wondered, was she to have another? Was it possible they had found something? But no, it had been said so casually, with no hint of urgency. Perhaps it was just a shade too casual? Or was I being my usual pessimistic self?

The arrangements for the scan were made as we left the clinic and went to the car. I managed to make my awful suspicions known to Alan, as the girls rushed on ahead, eager to visit Demelza, and arguing over who was to give her the present we had brought with us.

'Don't be silly, it's just routine,' said Alan. 'After all, it's been six months since she had the last one.' It sounded so reasonable put like that. I realised that perhaps I was being over-anxious and tried to push the terrible thoughts to the back of my mind as we drove to the other hospital. On our arrival in the children's ward to visit Demelza and her parents, we were greeted by several of the nurses who had looked after Victoria. They joined the ranks of those greatly impressed by her new leg. (It was Victoria herself, who had christened it thus, although the 'new' had by now been dropped: artificial limb was such a mouthful.) They too had heard about it from Sally, the Physiotherapist who had been with us at Roehampton when it was fitted. I felt that it defied description. It was not until it was actually seen that its realistic qualities could be fully appreciated.

As we neared Demelza's bed, I was struck by how tiny she looked lying there. My heart went out to both her and her parents. She was a pretty little girl, with her long blonde hair splayed out on the pillow behind her and an impish grin on her face. The girls both gave her the present, which she accepted shyly.

We spent some time talking to her parents, going over what had happened to us and how we felt about it. We had gone through it all, and I think it does anyone good just to talk about things, even if no advice or physical help is offered. They helped us as well. It brought a certain amount of comfort to us all, to share our experiences, each knowing how the other felt.

Our attention, after a little while, was drawn to the

where the three girls had all been chatting quite happily, once the shyness had worn off. Victoria had been telling Demelza that she only had one leg, because she had had the very same operation.

'I don't believe you,' said Demelza indignantly, 'you've got two legs.'

Victoria explained to her that one of her legs was a 'pretend' one. But Demelza remained unconvinced.

'Shall I show her what it's like?' Victoria asked me.

'Yes, if you don't mind?'

She went right up to the bed and lifted up her skirt, so that Demelza could really see that the leg was indeed 'pretend'. That did the trick, and she was soon asking if she would be able to have one just like it.

Finally it was time to leave. We hadn't realised quite how late it was and the girls had to go to school in the morning. I think when we left the Spruces they didn't feel quite as despondent as they had before meeting Victoria. We promised to see them again the following week, when we brought Victoria in for the scan.

By the time the date for the scan arrived, I had managed to convince myself that Alan had been right and I had worried unnecessarily. Alan, rather than I, again went into the suite where the scanner was housed because of the weight of the lead apron. I did not have to wait as long as the last time, as it was only the upper abdomen that they were concerned with.

As we left I asked the Radiographer how long the results would take to come through. She thought about three or four days, by the time they had been collated by the two Consultants. They would be sure to let us know straight away.

We continued upstairs to the children's ward to see

Demelza as arranged. When we entered the ward, Sally and one of the nurses were by her bed. Looking up and seeing Victoria, Sally called out, 'Ah, here's my friend Victoria. How are you? I'll be with you in a minute.'

Before Victoria had a chance to reply a little voice piped up from the bed, 'She's not your friend, she's mine.'

'Oh, I'm sorry,' replied Sally, 'but she's my friend too, you know. Can't she be both our friends'?

'I suppose so,' came the rather reluctant reply, 'but she's my friend first.'

'Well, hurry up and let me put this on, and then we can both talk to our friend.'

The curtains had now been drawn round the bed and we had seen in Sally's hand a piece of Tubi-Grip which she was obviously trying to persuade the little girl to put on. Tubi-Grip is rather like a very thick white elastic stocking, without any of the leg shaping, made in various widths to give support. Now that the stitches were out, it would help to support the still tender wound. Victoria still wore it, as she found it more comfortable than pants. Several wails of protest issued from behind the drawn curtains.

'But I don't want it on,' Demelza firmly announced.

'It'll be much more comfortable for you,' said Sally, then, remembering their joint friend, 'Victoria had to wear it, you know.' Had this done the trick? There was a slight pause, before Demelza's voice was heard again, 'Did she?' She was obviously thinking it over. But it was no good. 'Well, *I'm* not going to, I don't like it.' She had thought about it and she was adamant. She was not going to wear it. Victoria and I looked at one another, smiling. She was trying not to laugh. 'Shall I go and show her that

I still wear it now?' she said.

'That's a good idea, if you don't mind. It might make her change her mind.'

She disappeared behind the curtains around the bed. There was a few minutes' silence while she unstrapped the leg to show off the Tubi-Grip. Then in no time at all the feat had been accomplished with no further complaints from Demelza and a conspiratorial wink from Sally, as she pulled back the curtains.

Kevin and Angela Spruce had now come into the ward. I mentioned that I had just noticed that Demelza had one of the newspaper pictures of Victoria with Sefton taped to the top of her bed. They explained that one of the nurses had put it there when she had first come in. On hearing all this, Victoria related her bargain with Corporal-Major Brown, and decided that when she did write to him, she would tell him about Demelza and ask him if she could bring her too. Demelza was thrilled by this prospect, and hoped that she too would have her 'New Leg' when the time came.

We didn't think we would be able to get in to see her again before she was discharged the following week, so we exchanged telephone numbers and addresses with Kevin and Angela and promised to keep in touch.

Joanna of course was furious when she heard about the visit and the fact that she had not seen Demelza because she had been at school. It was very difficult for her to understand that if she missed too much at school she would fall far behind the rest of her class. Particularly as Victoria had missed a great deal. It was not easy to strike a happy medium between trying to include Joanna in as much as we could, so as not to create any jealousy, and also to make sure she led a life that was as normal as possible for a child of her age. She soon got over her disappointment and thankfully it was the only time we had any problems in that direction.

During the days that followed the scan, I tried to keep myself as busy as possible, wondering all the time when we would hear anything, but no matter what I did, the time seemed to drag. Should I phone the hospital? No. Really, I was making far too much of it.

By the fourth day, however, I could stand it no longer, and breaking my resolve to wait until we were contacted, I phoned Mr Steel's secretary. She explained that as the results had to be seen by two different Consultants, who were in two different hospitals, the results might take a little longer than usual. She would tell Mr Steel that I had called and ask him to ring me as soon as he heard anything at all.

Victoria had not gone to school on this particular day because she had been feeling unwell recently. This compounded my fears even further and added to my now desperate need to know the results of the scan, especially as one of the things she had complained of was a slight pain in her lower ribs on the left side. Was it her lungs? Oh don't be so stupid, I kept telling myself.

When the telephone rang later in the afternoon, I managed to conquer my first impulse to answer immediately. It might not even be the hospital anyway.

'Mrs Hart?' asked the voice on the other end of the line. I recognised it immediately as being that of Mr Steel's secretary.

'Yes,' I answered feebly, my heart in my mouth as I waited to hear what she had to say.

'Mr Steel would like to see both you and your husband tomorrow at two o'clock. Will that be all right?'

I managed to answer that it would, all the time thinking that all my morbid thoughts had been true. They had found something. Terrified that Victoria might overhear what I said, I struggled to manoeuvre the phone from its usual place in the hall into the sitting room and close the door. 'You will both be coming, won't you?' reiterated the voice on the phone.

'Yes, we will.' I don't even remember whether I said goodbye or not. I was so stunned. I hadn't wanted to admit even to myself that there could really be something wrong. How could I tell Alan? What would we say to Victoria? With supreme effort I replaced the phone and managed to control myself sufficiently to go upstairs. In answer to Victoria's question, 'Who was that on the phone?' I lied by saying it had just been a friend whom I hadn't seen for some time.

'I'm getting up now. My headache's gone and Joanna will be home from school soon.'

No mention of the pain in her side. In a daze, I managed to find her clothes. Perhaps I was still worrying unnecessarily. She seemed fine now. But then why had he asked specifically to see us both? I really didn't know what to think. I couldn't even get in touch with Alan. If I started ringing round to try and find out where he and his father were working, Victoria was sure to become suspicious. I would just have to wait until he came home.

I managed to muddle through the rest of the afternoon, giving the girls their tea when Joanna got in from school, and starting to prepare the evening meal. Luckily, Alan finished early that night for some reason and came in shortly after Joanna.

I followed him upstairs as he went to get changed. The

118

girls were engrossed in the television, so hadn't noticed my exit. He was as stunned as I had been—the more so as he had been the one to try and convince me that the scan had only been routine. Neither of us was convinced of that now. What should we tell Victoria? Nothing yet, we decided. We told them that we had to go and see the bank manager about some business and that Alan's mother would pick them up from school because we didn't know how long we would be. If we had told her that we were going to see Mr Steel, she would certainly have guessed that something was wrong.

Later that evening, after the girls were in bed, Alan and I sat and talked for ages. It seemed all too recently that we had done this before. Neither of us felt much like sleeping though. We tried to convince ourselves that it would turn out not to be as serious as we both feared and that she could be treated successfully with chemo-therapy. We knew that any more radiotherapy was out of the question at the moment. It was only four months since the post-operative course had finished. I said that perhaps we should imagine the results being the worst that they could possibly be, so that it would be a bonus when the truth was not as bad as we had feared. Who was I kidding?

It was with heavy hearts that we eventually decided that, although sleep would probably not come, we ought to try to rest. We would need all our strength. Tomorrow might prove to be quite an ordeal.

I lay awake for hours. Why did it have to happen? After the way Victoria had coped with the amputation it seemed so wrong that she might have to go through something even more unpleasant. Why, oh why did it have to be her? Life can be very cruel and for no apparent reason. She had never done anything to harm anyone. It really wasn't fair. I found it extremely hard to keep my faith at that moment but it was stronger than I thought and never let me down.

# CHAPTER
## 11

In the corridor outside Mr Steel's office, Alan and I saw Sally waiting for us. She greeted us cheerfully enough, but it was obvious she was there for moral support. Perhaps even to help us cope with what we were about to hear? It was hard to carry on a normal conversation. Our hearts just weren't in it. All we could think about was what we would be told when we actually went in to see Mr Steel.

At last he called us into his office. Although it was only a few minutes after our arrival, we seemed to have been waiting for an eternity. One look at his face as we sat down was enough to confirm our fears. There was something terribly wrong. Dear God, please don't let it be too bad.

He seemed loath to begin. We both sensed that he was finding it very difficult to know how to start, as he shuffled through the various papers that were in front of him. We held on tight to each other's hands. He cleared his throat. A distant door banged, but apart from that you could have heard a pin drop.

'I'm sure you must have realised that something is wrong,' he began, 'and I'm afraid that the scan has confirmed what we suspected from the chest X-ray at the clinic. The cancer has spread to her lungs.' He paused, as if to collect his thoughts, or to give us time to realise fully what he had said. We clasped each other's hands tighter, as if in some way it would help to stave off some of the awful feeling of despair. '. . . I'm afraid it looks very bad. It has spread to both lungs. Apart from three main tumours, there are widespread spots as well.' I couldn't control the tears that had started. What was he saying? It couldn't be true? Not Victoria. No. No. I wanted to scream, tell me it's not true.

'I just cannot believe it,' he said despondently, 'I mean for it to return so quickly and to be so widespread, after the way she's taken it all. I really don't know what to say. It makes me wonder whether I should even have done the amputation in the first place. She'd taken it all so well—and now this.'

'Oh no, you mustn't think that,' I said, alarmed at the despair in his voice. Was he really telling us that there was no hope? Surely not. Why? After all she had gone through? All I could think, was why, why, why?

Alan's voice broke through my thoughts, as I heard him ask whether or not chemotherapy would cure her. Yes, perhaps my thoughts had been a little hasty. Mr Steel explained that naturally he had spoken to the Consultant Radiologist, and treatment had been discussed.

'But of course one has to decide whether the treatment will be worse for her to endure than the disease itself.'

What he was saying was that as there was not much chance of curing the cancer, why put her through a painful and unpleasant course of drug treatment as well? Why make her totally miserable and uncomfortable?

We steeled ourselves as Alan asked the one question to which we both dreaded the answer, but nevertheless had to know.

'What are her chances of being cured with the treatment?'

There was a light pause before he answered. We could both see that he was finding it extremely difficult, especially as he had become so fond of Victoria over the last few months.

'I'm sorry to have to say that apart from the treatment she needs a miracle.'

We were completely and utterly devastated. Although we had both kidded ourselves that we would imagine the worst, it had been impossible. How can one possibly imagine that one's own beloved ten-year-old daughter is going to die?

We sat with our arms around each other, hardly able to control our tears. What words can express the way we both felt? Nobody could ever have prepared us to cope with what we were now faced. We just couldn't believe it was really happening, that it was really true. Mr Steel got up to leave, saying he had another appointment, but we could see how upset he was.

'You are welcome to stay here as long as you like. I simply can't express how sorry I am, and, believe me, I know how inadequate that must sound to you,' he said, going on to explain that it was out of his sphere now and that any form of treatment would be dealt with by the cancer specialist and his registrar.

We could see how shattered he was, but at the same time we knew that he had wanted to be the one to tell us. As he had said, it was out of his sphere now, and should normally have been dealt with by the cancer specialists.

We will always be very grateful to him for that. We knew how hard it must have been for him, and yet it was something he had done through choice, and not because he had to.

For a while after he left we just sat there, holding onto each other, neither speaking nor moving. What was there to say? Where could we go? We were in no fit state to return home just yet.

Sally came into the room to see how we were. Would we like a cup of coffee? Or would we prefer just to be left on our own? We had a few words with her. We didn't want to be rude, but I think she sensed that we wanted to be on our own, and she left after only a few minutes.

After some time we realised that we couldn't stay there forever. We had to pull ourselves together. Making a supreme effort to appear as normal as possible, we made our way to Alan's parents' house to pick up the girls. They would not have to be told yet, not until we knew the time of our appointment at the cancer clinic. It would be impossible for us to convey any of what we had been told to Mum and Dad with Victoria and Joanna there. On the pretext of having forgotten to give his father some building plans he needed, Alan went back to see them later in the evening as the girls were going to bed, and they thought nothing of it.

It was going to be even more difficult this time to carry on normally. How could we possibly hide the way we were feeling? But it was amazing how much easier it turned out to be than we had thought. It was especially so in front of the girls who were always so bright and cheerful that it was impossible to be too down-hearted. It was different of course when they were at school and we were on our own; then we talked of nothing else.

We felt we had been given a special strength to cope with it all, although there was still the nagging dilemma in our minds of reconciling what we are told of a loving God with one who could so abruptly end a young life. It all seemed so senseless and unfair. Where was the reason? Would we ever know? But in the end Victoria herself served to strengthen my belief. It was the way she rose above despair that helped us to be strong, the way she trusted her life so completely to others, and by that I don't just mean to all the doctors and nurses but to us, her family, and, as she put it, to Jesus. It was this simple faith that I'm sure helped her in a way that people could not. And it was a simple faith which I'm sure some might term a blind faith. But it was nevertheless there, intangible, although she never wanted or felt the need to go to church.

We heard that our appointment with the cancer specialist was to be in two days' time. That time was spent in a kind of limbo, so reminiscent of the other time, just six short months ago. The worst feeling was one of complete and utter helplessness, not knowing what form the treatment would take, or even when it would start. Then came the feeling that we couldn't just sit there and let it just happen. There must surely be something we could do, there must be some form of treatment somewhere that would give us more hope than we had at the moment. Two days seemed such a long time to us. We wanted to know everything right now, this minute. Alan decided to telephone the Consultant. Perhaps we would be able to see him sooner. He was very kind and explained much that we wanted to know over the phone, and although it was impossible for the appointment to be brought forward, we were welcome to phone him any time. One tends to forget at such times that there are many other patients waiting to be seen, all just as important as ourselves. He restated the point that Mr Steel had made, that they did not want the treatment itself to cause more misery and discomfort than the cancer. Alan asked about the possibility of surgery. But that was out of the question at this stage due to the fact that the cancer was so widespread, but it might be a possibility if the chemotherapy reduced it considerably. What about lung transplants? We had heard that these had been tried in the States. This too was out of the question; they were still in their infancy and were usually performed in conjunction with heart transplants. Alan also mentioned that we had finally booked our long awaited holiday abroad for the beginning of June. We were both horrified when he advised us to bring the date forward. It was only four months away, surely we would have longer than that? I couldn't believe it. Alan kept pressing him for some indication of her chances of recovery. He was reluctant to do this and perhaps we were being a little unfair in insisting on knowing, but we felt that we had a right to know. We were devastated to know that he estimated her chances at about one per cent. Was there nothing that anyone could do? We couldn't just helplessly watch her die.

It was with all this in mind that we contacted our family doctor. He, too, was very kind. We hadn't known him very long, having changed doctors because of our move. He agreed to come to the house to speak to us when the girls were at school. We asked him if we could see someone else, seek another opinion, not that we doubted what we had been told, but we had to satisfy ourselves (as we had at the time of the amputation) that all that could be done was in fact being done. There had been much publicity recently, only that week as it happened, about micro-surgery and how it had been used to cure brain tumours in America for two British children after which it transpired that the operation could have been done in this country. We didn't want anything like that to happen, although we knew that even micro-surgery was out of the question. Brain tumours were after all very different from Victoria's cancer. We just had to know of any possibilities, however remote. We realised after seeing the doctor that there was no other choice, but he agreed to make an appointment for a second opinion with a specialist at the Royal Marsden Hospital in London.

As Alan and I talked endlessly over and over what we already knew and speculated as to what we didn't and what was to come, we came to question the most important fact: that any treatment or indeed surgery, if it were possible, must be to help Victoria, and not just to make us feel better about having tried everything. This was brought home to me when a friend, on hearing the awful news, had said, 'Well, of course, one would try absolutely anything to save one's child.'

But what of the quality of that life? We felt that had to be given a great deal of consideration. To take her halfway across the world in the vague hope that some new and unproven form of surgery might cure her was a risk we were not prepared to take. Would it not be much worse if she died in some strange country? Among people she didn't know? We had no right to play God, just so that we could say, well, we tried everything we could, didn't we? What right had we to put her through anything that was going to be so much worse than the disease itself? And which could still leave her with no chance of life at the end of it all?

For this reason I was even sceptical of the chemotherapy she would undergo, having read so many of the horror stories connected with it; the loss of hair, sickness and complete debilitation in some cases.

This was the only time throughout all that had happened that Alan and I came even remotely close to disagreement over Victoria's treatment. I was unsure as to whether we should put her through what might, at the very least, I felt, be a traumatic experience. But how could I deny her the chance of life? No matter that it was so remote. As it turned out, and I thank God for it, my worst fears were never realised, much to the relief of all concerned. My mind would go back to a phrase which has been used by many at the time of the amputation, myself included, 'When one door closes, another one opens.' Why did I now feel that the door had been firmly slammed shut in my face? But even now, in the face of everything we had been told, there was still hope, the chance that she would be the one to prove them all wrong. That she *would* be that one per cent.

Alan and I had a long discussion with the doctor who would be in charge of her case. Dr Jane Martin. It was she who would prescribe the drugs, and that really was the only chance she had, and a chance we had to take. She explained absolutely everything to Alan, even going as far as to show him some of the scans and X-rays. She told him that not every patient suffers the hair loss or the sickness, but that we ought to prepare ourselves and Victoria for this when the time came, as she was to be given the strongest possible dose for a child of her age. The doctor couldn't say for certain, however, exactly

On holiday in Spain, June 1983

A treasured memory always

how the effects would manifest themselves.

Alan certainly felt much more hopeful after he had seen Dr Martin. I was more pessimistic. I knew how Victoria felt about her hair and how she hated being sick. But it was Victoria herself who, with her quiet faith and courage, opened the door we felt to have been so firmly shut. She stunned and inspired all who met her, and in the words of Dr Martin, 'She reacted to it all with a sense of philosophical understanding, always calm and serene and without any fuss whatsoever.'

We had decided for the time being at least not to do anything about bringing our holiday forward. It was as if by actually changing the date, we would hasten things in some way.

We went to the clinic as planned, telling Victoria it was just for a checkup. But she knew. She always seemed to know more than any of us gave her credit for. She thought it odd that she should have another checkup so soon after the last one. We had always said from the beginning that we would never tell her any lies, but only as much as we wanted her to know at any one time. We were therefore stunned when, on the way back home, she said, 'Well, perhaps they have found something from the scan and I'l have to have some treatment. But I don't want another operation.'

We told her that we didn't know as yet exactly what had shown on the scan, but that she was to see a professor in London the following week. I assured her that I felt sure she wouldn't have to have an operation.

The trip to the Royal Marsden only confirmed what we had already been told, although the specialist seemed slightly more optimistic about the outcome of the treatment. We felt it had been well worth going, as we were now convinced there was hope and that the worst thing we could do was to give up.

Later that evening, after I had kissed Joanna and settled her down for the night, I made my way into Victoria's room. She asked me to sit on the bed. This was nothing unusual as she often liked to have a little chat at bedtime, when she had me on my own, but I could sense that this was something more than a little chat. Out of the blue, she said, 'Mummy, am I going to die?' She had said it quite calmly, with no hint of fear in her voice. What could I say? This was going to be a real test of our policy of only telling the truth.

'What makes you say that?'

'I don't know really. I don't want to die, but a lot of people who have cancer do die, don't they? Remember that programme on telly about that boy who had his leg amputated?' Yes, I did remember. It had been a documentary about Terry Fox, a young Canadian who, after an amputation, had undertaken a marathon across Canada, raising many thousands of pounds for cancer research. Sadly he had died before completing the marathon. Fancy Victoria remembering the programme.

'Well, he died, didn't he?'

'Yes, he did. But look at Bob Champion. He had cancer and not only was he cured but he went on to win the Grand National.'

'I don't mind having the treatment, not really, it's just that I don't want to lose my hair.' A natural reaction and I'm sure I would have felt the same.

'But I'm not having another operation. I won't need it anyway.' She was quite adamant about that.

'Well, I don't think you'll have to and you might not lose your hair. It doesn't happen to everyone. Why don't you ask the doctor yourself when we go tomorrow? You must never worry about things on your own.' I tried to reassure her, but I felt guilty at having sounded so optimistic in doing so. But how could I have been anything else with one so young, particularly one as perceptive as Victoria?

She now knew, of course, that she was to have treatment and that tomorrow's appointment was to discuss when it would begin. She would also undergo a liver scan and a blood test, to make sure that everything was in order beforehand. I gave her a big hug as she lay down to sleep. 'Well, Jesus will look after me, he did the last time.' This was a statement rather than a question and I left the room somewhat comforted by the way in which she was taking it all. I gained strength from her strength, and faith from her faith. I knew then that no matter what happened or what the outcome might be, she would never be frightened by anything that was to come.

# CHAPTER
## 12

It was now the first week in March and the date set for Victoria's first course of treatment. I couldn't help thinking that a month had already passed since the scan. If the cancer had suddenly developed from almost nothing to what had appeared in the scan in just three months, how much further could it have spread even in one month? But she had had a chest X-ray the previous day, and nothing had been mentioned.

The liver scan and the blood test had both proved to be fine and so the treatment, which would take thirty hours to complete, could commence. We had to be at the children's ward by nine o'clock. Victoria had been allowed to come to the children's ward because she was familiar with it and knew the staff, although the treatment was normally carried out at the other part of the district hospital. She was pleased to see all the nurses again and feeling so much at home there helped to dispel any worries she might have had. Sadly Jill, who had been one of her favourites, had left the hospital some months earlier to take up a post as Sister in the special baby-care unit of another hospital. But Victoria still saw her and her husband from time to time, and they knew what had happened.

The doctor was about to insert into the back of her hand the needle for the intravenous drip through which the drug would be administered. Victoria held my hand very tightly as the needle went in. She didn't flinch as the tubing from the polythene bag containing the drug was connected to the needle and the yellow coloured liquid was soon flowing through.

The drug is a poison and consequently has to be introduced into the body quickly and flushed out immediately, before it can do too much harm to any of the normal cells. It was important that Victoria drank as much as possible to help this process, and to this end had already had to drink at least two litres of liquid during the previous two days at home. Once the drug had passed through her body, the bag was changed to one containing an ordinary saline solution, again to help flush the drug through. A different drug was added to this at six-hourly intervals, also to counter the effects of the first drug. This process was continued at home in tablet form, though still at six-hourly intervals, until the full cycle of sixty hours was complete. Blood samples too were taken at regular intervals, to make sure that the drug was not having an adverse effect.

We were not the only ones to be concerned as to how Victoria would react to the drugs. The doctors were frequently asking her how she felt and apart from feeling a little tired, she seemed to be suffering no ill-effects at all. We were all so relieved that she didn't feel any of the sickness we had anticipated. Apart from the slight handicap caused by the splint, to keep the hand with the needle in it immobile, she seemed fine and was able to amuse herself by drawing or playing games with Alan and me.

Victoria still wondered, and so did I, about her hair, but no-one could tell us about that for certain. We would just have to wait and see. She amused us all by inspecting the pillow at intervals to make sure it was not already falling out. I sent up a silent prayer that she would be spared that. Surely, all things considered, that was such a little thing to ask.

Three days after the treatment had started saw Victoria getting ready to go back to school. No-one was going to stop her, despite the fact that she still had to drink at least two litres of liquid during the next twenty-four hours. She went armed with a huge bottle of ready diluted squash, as well as her usual bag of books and pencils. We had already been to the school to see the headmistress and to tell her of our dreadful news, explaining what the treatment might involve. She had been very upset. She was very fond of Victoria and used to call her 'My little girl'. Yet again, she proved to be a great source of comfort to us and said that she would not yet tell any of the staff too much, in case it was discussed in the staff-room and leaked out in some way. It is strange looking back that although we never at any time planned what we would say to various people who asked, it became so easy to answer questions about Victoria's necessary absences from school, without arousing any undue suspicion. This even extended to her being accused of 'skiving' which she felt was most unfair, and which I was furious about. I suppose this resulted from her being absent from school for about four days out of ten, and of course the rest of the children didn't know why, although she did tell them she had to go to the hospital. I found it hard to understand that they had not discussed it with their parents, most of whom knew by now, and been told why. But children can be so forth-right and at times so cruel. However, it was soon forgotten and would have caused even more problems had I made a fuss about it, although I certainly felt like doing so.

She had been reminded, on leaving the hospital after that first treatment, that if she felt at all unwell, even the very slightest hint of a sore throat, she *must* tell us, so that we could bring her in for a blood test to make sure that there was nothing seriously wrong, to be sure that the drug wasn't causing any harm.

Whether it was the thought of the blood test or not (she would never get used to the needles), I don't know, but I could see that after two days she was worried about something. As she watched television, obviously think-ing I wasn't noticing, her hand would feel round her throat. 'Are you all right?' I asked. 'Yes, of course I am. Why did you ask?' She realised that I was constantly on the watch for anything that might indicate something untoward.

'You must tell me, you know, even if you think it's nothing. It's best to make sure,' I said. Silence for a few seconds, then she said,

'Well, it's just my throat feels a little, well, sort of dry. It's not really sore. Honestly, it's nothing.' What should I do? They had told us that even the very slightest hint of a sore throat should alert us to bring her in. Knowing too that she rarely admitted to any pain, I told Alan that I thought we ought at least to contact the hospital to see what they thought.

To be on the safe side Sister Ford of the children's ward felt that we should bring her in for a blood test. This was duly accomplished to the satisfaction of all concerned, apart from Victoria. She was furious about the whole thing. 'I told you it was nothing.' I'm sure even if her throat had been really sore she would have made light of it. As it turned out, we were able to return home with our minds at rest. And Victoria did eventually realise how necessary it all was.

The treatment was to be carried out every ten days but not until the results of the initial blood test had come back to show that all was well and the drugs were doing no harm to the rest of her system. Although she didn't particularly look forward to these visits to the hospital, she didn't complain and was soon instructing any new junior nurse in the operation of the intravenous equipment. The fact that she never felt any ill effects of course helped a great deal. It might have been very different had this not been so. We would certainly have felt a lot more anguish on her behalf. One of us taking it in turns to stay overnight at the hospital with her helped, so that Joanna was not left with anyone else. All this helped things to go as smoothly as possible.

There were several amusing incidents that kept us all going, and Victoria used to get away with quite a lot as far as the nurses were concerned. Like pressing the buzzer (only once, I might add) to call a nurse because she knew it would be one in particular who joked with her, and pretending she had seen an air bubble in the tubing of the drip. She knew small air bubbles would do no harm, but she didn't like them.

The liquid intake and output during the course of the treatment was constantly monitored. What went in was measured, and so was what came out, which caused a great deal of amusement to Victoria. Considering the quantities she had to drink, I'll leave it to your imagination as to what the end products amounted to.

When she was about three weeks into her treatment, Victoria could talk of nothing but the forthcoming gymnastics display at school, which was to take place just before the end of term. There were going to be medals presented for the best under eight years and the best under eleven years old. Victoria's class were all hoping it would be won by one of them, Emma, who as far as I could discern seemed to be made of india rubber.

But what of Victoria? Would she be able to take part? She would only have completed that week's treatment the day before the display and would still be taking certain drugs. Surely it was going to be impossible? The situation was resolved when Dr Martin found out about it and arranged for the treatment to start two days earlier than planned. There was never any question that perhaps she shouldn't take part. There was never any doubt when there were physical activities she wished to do. The doctors felt it was important for her wellbeing to do the things she enjoyed doing. Another indication perhaps, that she hadn't long? So why spoil her enjoyment of life as well as making her suffer the treatment?

We had certainly not given up hope. After the first two courses of treatment had been carried out, the chest X-ray prior to the next visit had shown that although one of the larger tumours had increased slightly in size, the smaller and more widespread spots had disappeared. This raised our hopes enormously and consequently we still did nothing about bringing our holiday forward. This was partly because we had been considering the possibility of taking the girls to Disneyland instead of Spain, as we had originally planned. But we decided against this. For one thing, Victoria was sure to wonder how, suddenly, we were able to afford such an extravagant holiday. Secondly we could imagine nothing worse than her being taken very ill when we were such a long way from home and from all the doctors and nurses whom she knew well and trusted, and who in turn knew her. So the holiday in Spain remained provisionally booked for the second Thursday in June.

The only person to have shown any anxiety towards Victoria's part in the gym display had been Sally, and then only because she could see how terrible it would be if she injured her leg. When Victoria asked her if she would like to come to school and watch, Sally hadn't shown her that she was at all worried, but instead had made a joke of it by saying, 'Victoria, I'm afraid I would need a bottle of tranquillisers to be able to watch you.' She did happen to be working anyway and Victoria thought the reference to the tranquillisers a huge joke. But I have to admit I shared Sally's nervousness. The only person to remain completely unconcerned about the whole thing was Victoria. Even Joanna was agitated; games and sports were not her forte.

On the appointed day we met Alan's parents at the entrance to the gym hall which was already quite full, but we managed to find seats near the front. I was feeling very nervous by this time on Victoria's behalf. I don't know why I should have been though. She most certainly wasn't.

The display began with the kindergarten class, most of them barely five years old. They were very sweet as they skipped around the hall and they managed to do some very good 'bunny-hops'. When Joanna's class came on to show off their skills, I suddenly realised that I'd forgotten to bring the camera. Typical, I thought, but was comforted by the fact that I could see one or two parents I knew who were obviously not as absent-minded as myself. Joanna managed to perform everything at least as well as the rest of her class and I was pleased for her. She was a sturdily built child and although not really fat she put up with rather a lot of ribbing, mainly from her sister.

It was hard to concentrate on the efforts of the younger classes. All I could think about was how Victoria would cope when her turn came? Would it start to worry her that there was a large audience—not just her school friends that she had been used to? I felt sure I would never have been able to do it, had I been in her position. It served to highlight just how she felt about it all. She had had a leg amputated, but she was still the same person as before and was determined to carry on exactly as she had previously. To us she was of course always Victoria, not Victoria with only one leg.

At last it was her class's turn. My heart skipped a beat as they entered the hall, one behind the other, taking a few steps and rolling a forward somersault. Looking at Victoria, as she did all that the other girls did, I found it hard to believe that she did only have one leg. They went on to do some exercises using the box and the bars, and last of all and the most amazing to us, the ropes. This was the surprise she had been keeping from us, I thought as I recalled her unwillingness to give any details of what she would actually be doing, when we had asked. The girls each held a vertically hung rope in either hand and did various exercises with only the ropes for support, including turning right over and remaining upside down for some seconds. The performance confirmed in our minds how wrong it would have been for any of us to have stopped her from doing what she so obviously enjoyed which, despite the apprehension of others, she went on to do without apparent difficulty, proving that any such fears held on her behalf were, as she had thought, groundless.

Now that the display was over, the time came for the medals to be presented. This was accompanied by a great deal of cheering from the children as the winners were announced, particularly as the senior medal was awarded, as they had hoped, to Emma. It had obviously been the most popular choice. When I heard the next few words of Mrs Barnes the gym mistress, tears of pride and happiness sprang to my eyes.

'And now for a young lady who despite having been through what to most of us adults would have been a devastating experience, has carried on in a way that would daunt many, without any complaint or wish for special treatment or consideration. That must surely be a lesson to us all. I would like to ask Victoria Hart to come up and receive this special medal.'

Victoria seemed stunned. I watched her friends congratulate her and she seemed not to realise what had happened. Then she got up to collect her medal. She hopped up so gracefully, her face wreathed in smiles now as she accepted that the loud applause was for her.

It was a marvellous and proud day for us all. Alan's parents were so pleased that we had asked them to come with us. Joanna was very proud of her sister and Victoria was surprised that she had a medal, and justifiably proud of it. I could see that many of the parents had been very moved and several told us what an edifying experience they felt it to be. Although they had heard from their own daughters that she would be taking part in the display, they had never imagined that she would do so well and with such confidence. This was another facet of her character that never ceased to amaze us, her family. She had been rather shy and retiring before, rather overshadowed to some extent by Joanna's more extrovert personality. But she had imperceptibly changed, though she never in any way showed off or made a display of false modesty. There was certainly something different about her. Had we been asked what this was, I doubt that we would have been able to define it. She seemed to have an inner tranquillity and serenity which became more marked as the weeks passed, something about her that was to us indeed special.

During her next visit to the hospital for treatment, the week after the display, she was not to be separated from her medal. Mr Steel came up to see her, as he often did if he knew she was in the ward when he happened to be doing his rounds. He was thrilled by her achievement and asked her to put the medal on to show him. Alan and I felt that from the start he had played no small part in it all, with his words of encouragement to her.

The school term finished just before Easter, which brought its usual and very welcome supply of chocolate eggs, devoured with great enthusiasm. We spent the holiday period on our own. We were becoming rather selfish with our time as a family, needing to be alone, and although we still accepted the odd invitation, these were not frequent, as most of our friends realised how we felt and respected our need.

The treatment was continuing almost weekly with no change, but at least it was becoming no worse, so we were able to keep on hoping. I should mention, perhaps, that my parents remained unaware of what was happening to their eldest granddaughter. We had decided, combined with the advice of others, that we would divulge nothing for the time being. Although they had taken the amputation very well, living so far away Mum especially would have wanted to rush straight down to see Victoria, which would only have served to arouse Victoria's suspicions. I felt rather bad about it, more so during the first phone call after we had been told the awful truth. In reply to Mum's usual question I had assured her gaily that Victoria was fine. I found that having said so once it didn't seem quite so bad thereafter. Sheila of course knew, as did Alan's sister and her husband, though not their children.

Towards the end of April we suffered a setback. The drugs, because of their frequency, had begun to have an adverse affect on Victoria's liver. It was described to us as much the same as the effect of alcohol after a heavy night's drinking. We had been warned that there was a chance of this happening. It meant she was unable to have further chemotherapy for at least ten days. Perhaps more. This was a considerable blow to everyone, although not entirely unexpected. We had to take her weekly to the clinic for the chest X-ray and blood test, and ten days after her last treatment the X-ray showed that one of the tumours had grown quite markedly. The doctors decided to give her one fairly strong dose of radiotherapy, as her liver had not recovered sufficiently to allow further chemotherapy. Another shield was made. Victoria had grown since the last time, but it didn't take as long to make this one. The treatment seemed to knock her out, and once we got home she slept for most of the afternoon. She had started to cough, not very much, but enough to worry us.

We had always made it clear to Dr Martin that we

wanted to be told everything. We wanted nothing kept from us, no matter how upsetting it might prove to be. For this reason, Alan and I both went with Victoria to the clinic as well as staying in the hospital with her, so that one of us would remain with her while the other could speak to the doctor. She was slightly suspicious of this practice at first, but we explained to her that the doctors sometimes used words to us that she wouldn't have understood and that might have worried her. We assured her that we would always tell her what had been said. I wouldn't want anyone to think that she was being given the impression that nothing much was wrong and that she would soon be better. She was a very sick little girl. She knew that she felt worse and only she knew how bad the pain was. But the last thing we wanted was for her to be frightened in any way, and we took care that she never was. We still think we were right in this. You cannot go up to a child and say, 'Look, I'm sorry, but you're going to die.' I'm sure she knew herself anyway because she talked about dying and whether people went to hell, as if she were trying to come to terms with it. I think she probably helped us more than we helped her, not that she was constantly talking about dying, only now and then.

Thankfully, the week after the radiotherapy her liver recovered and the drug treatment could begin again. The Summer term had started the week previously and Victoria had joined the others in returning her form for the sponsored walk. She had already taken it into the hospital and collared as many of the doctors and nurses as she could to put their money on her. None of us could quite believe that she actually meant to go ahead with it, what with the treatment and her cough which was a little worse. But she carried on in her own quietly determined way, making it clear no-one was going to stop her.

She would only be released from the hospital the day before the walk. Would she be able to take part? But she was adamant, especially as she had so many signatures on her form and planned to raise over a hundred pounds on her own. Dr Martin agreed to her taking part on condition that Alan and I went with her. I had imagined that one of us would accompany her anyway, and it was to prove no great hardship. After all, Victoria was going to do it, and there was nothing wrong with either of *us*.

# CHAPTER
## 13
---

For the three days and nights before the sponsored walk it rained continually. The route through farmland and woods was more like an army assault course than a walk with a convent school! The going was very tough, with the mud ankle deep in some places. Victoria carried on, as usual, undaunted despite still taking drugs which we administered along the way, although Alan had to lift her over some of the deeper mud patches. I could just imagine the reaction at Roehampton, had they known. I lost one of my wellingtons twice by getting stuck in the mud, much to Victoria's amusement.

It was only when we had reached the six mile stage of the twelve that had been set that Victoria was finally persuaded to call it a day. She was by then in some pain, but would never have admitted it. It was left to us to guess and ask if she wanted anything for it. Pain-killers were more often than not declined. She had done exceptionally well. There were one or two who had given up earlier because of the muddy conditions. Everyone was struck by her courage and tenacity in even taking part.

The local paper published an article the following

week on her efforts, having sent a photographer to cover the start. The school received a number of donations from complete strangers once the paper was in the shops.

The newspaper article also brought Victoria to the attention of a lady called Margaret, also known as Mrs 'Fix-It'. As her nickname suggests, she got to hear about sick children, found out if there was someone they really wanted to meet and then arranged it all for them. She phoned us to say that she had made arrangements for another little girl to see Cannon and Ball in Crawley the following Sunday, but she was now too ill to go. Would Victoria like to go instead? Would she! Both she and Joanna had always liked this comic twosome. So it was all fixed.

We thoroughly enjoyed the show. I can't remember when I had last laughed so much, they were hilarious. The biggest excitement was when we were taken backstage to meet them afterwards. They were super with Victoria. She and Joanna were slightly in awe of them at first, but managed to ask them for a signed photo, and when Victoria had hers taken with them, I could see that they were impressed by her. A remark from Bobby Ball still sticks in my memory; 'And to think that my daughter complains if she has a spot.' I think that summed it up for me.

We had kept in touch with Demelza and her parents, as we had promised. Unfortunately her father had happened to come into the ward one day while Victoria was having treatment. We hadn't told them that her condition had deteriorated, knowing it would worry them.

Victoria had at last kept her bargain and written to Corporal-Major Brown of the Household Cavalry, to tell him that she was now able to walk without her sticks.

She also asked if she might bring Demelza with her on her next visit, explaining that this little girl had undergone the same operation. She was over the moon to receive a reply, signed, 'Yours without stocks, Mike Brown.' The reason for her great excitement was that the envelope contained not only a reply to her letter but also official invitations, for all of us, Demelza's family too, to attend the ceremony of the presentation of new standards to the Household Cavalry, by Her Majesty The Queen on May 19 at Horse Guards. We could hardly believe it ourselves and thought of nothing else for the next few weeks.

We all had to have new outfits, and mine was the cause of much hilarity, from Victoria mostly, when they accompanied me to buy a new hat for the occasion. I managed to choose the one that caused the least amusement. The cloud on the horizon was the fact that Victoria's condition had become considerably worse. She was now breathing with difficulty which to her annoyance forced her into a wheelchair at times. She was also coughing much more, but still had to be persuaded into taking any pain-killers. She seemed to refuse to acknowledge pain. She wanted to carry on normally, although she couldn't attend school as much as she would have liked to.

We were asked again by the hospital if we had brought the holiday forward. The doctors felt this would be the wisest thing to do, especially as everyone felt that a holiday together at this point would be of far more benefit to us all than the treatment. It would be the last holiday we would ever have as a family of four. But we still didn't change it. I think in some strange way we were hoping against hope that the treatment would show some signs that it was having an effect, although knowing deep in our hearts that this would not be the case. However, we had just paid the full amount for the holiday and felt that if we were able to go it would be marvellous. If not, well, only time would tell.

At about this time Victoria received a letter from Major John Watson, a former officer in the Household Cavalry. He was now a writer, and his book about Sefton was due out at the beginning of July. He wrote to say that there was a photograph of her in it, taken when she had visited the barracks. Major Watson would be delighted to present her with a signed copy of the book if she would like one? Naturally she replied that she would love one and looked forward to seeing it.

This time we decided to stay in a hotel for the night before the ceremony, otherwise it would have meant such an early start from home on the morning itself. We would have arrived in our 'finery' looking as though we had slept in it. It would not be so tiring for Victoria either, staying in London the night before. We met Kevin, Angela and Demelza at the hotel, and spent a pleasant few hours with them after the girls had gone to bed, having drinks in the hotel bar, but decided not to stay up too long as we had an early start in the morning. The *Daily Mail* were going to cover the story, as were the BBC news team, and they had arranged to film at the barracks with Sefton at eight o'clock, before the parade. I could well imagine how the commanding officer might feel about that.

When we arrived, after a hurried breakfast, we spent much of the time apologising for causing them so much trouble before such an important occasion. But never was even a hint of inconvenience suggested and nothing was too much trouble for them, even providing us all with very welcome cups of coffee before it was time to leave. All this in the middle of their preparations. There were horses and riders everywhere getting ready to leave the barracks and make their way to the parade ground.

Victoria wanted the wheelchair, which we had been forced to bring with us, kept well in the background. Part of her bargain, she reminded me, was that she was supposed to be walking on her own. I had a quiet word with Corporal-Major Brown, well out of earshot of the press. The wheelchair was the last thing we wanted in the paper or on TV. He was stunned, thinking, as had many, that she had been cured. I tried to explain how much all that they were doing today meant to her, but it was hard to find the right words.

It was with a sense of unreality that we settled in our front row seats at Horse Guards, to await the arrival of Her Majesty The Queen who was to be accompanied by Her Royal Highness The Princess Anne. Demelza kept saying, 'When's she coming?' She caused a few smiles all round. I can only describe the occasion as fantastic, made even more memorable by the fact that the standard to be presented to the Blues and Royals was to replace the one torn to shreds by the IRA bombers the previous July. A stark reminder, as we watched it being trouped round Horse Guards, that there are enough horrors in the world without man creating any more.

It was wonderful to see the Queen and Princess Anne pass just in front of us in their open carriage. Victoria and Joanna were convinced that the Queen smiled just at them. It was a truly memorable day indeed and one that remains in our minds as clearly as ever, even now; something to treasure for the rest of our lives, made even more poignant by our realisation that had it not been for Victoria and her tremendous courage, we wouldn't have been invited to attend.

The press coverage was astonishing. The *Daily Mail* published a lovely photograph of Victoria and Demelza with Sefton, Demelza sitting astride him and Victoria at his head. The film on the BBC's news programme was lovely too, especially on John Craven's newsround. Or so I gathered. I missed it, due to the incessant ringing of our phone as soon as we arrived home. Everyone wanted to let us know that they had seen Victoria. It was before we had a video-recorder. The BBC kindly gave us a tape of the occasion, the same as the one they had used in their coverage, and we shall keep it always. The letters and phone calls continued for several days, making us aware that not only was Victoria an inspiration to us but to many others as well, people that we didn't even know. This was soon to be compounded in tragic circumstances.

# CHAPTER
## 14

The excitement of the trip to London was revived the following week at the hospital. The nurses had all either seen the coverage on TV or in the newspaper, and were all keen to see our photos and to hear all the details. We had even taken our precious video-recording to show those who had missed it. During that particular visit, it seemed that Victoria's bedside was always crowded with people anxious to see the recording again.

There was one special little person, whose visits Victoria greatly looked forward to. His name was Mark and he was just twelve weeks old. He had been in hospital for over three weeks because of an infection. His mother frequently brought him to Victoria's bed so that she could have a cuddle. She just adored him.

We met many children and their parents during our visits to the hospital. I think that without exception I would remember them today, mostly because of their kindness and sympathy, even in the face of their own children's suffering. Although we never volunteered information as to what was wrong with our daughter, we were sometimes asked. I suppose at other times people perhaps overhead snatches of conversation and put two put two and two together.

As the May Bank Holiday approached, we realised with rather a shock, that our holiday in Spain was only two weeks away. I could hardly believe it.

The Bank Holiday brought its own excitement. Linda and Jim (Alan's sister and her husband) with their four children, Jenny, Lisa, Natasha and Jamie were coming up to stay with Alan's parents. We had not seen any of them since that dreadful time last September when we had first discovered what was wrong with Victoria's knee. Lisa and Natasha were fairly close to our two in age, and they all got on extremely well. Jenny, fifteen, had grown out of the dressing-up games that the younger ones seemed to enjoy, but she still helped them in their games.

We enjoyed fabulous weather over the holiday and were able to have several barbecues. We had been concerned that Victoria might feel left out of all the fun. By now her breathing was very difficult. One lung had partially collapsed because of the size of the tumour, and, although she never complained, we knew that she was experiencing quite a lot of pain by now. I had caught her trying to hide tissues that were stained after a coughing fit on more than one occasion. She made light of it, reluctant still to take pain-killers.

I didn't know if Linda had spoken to her girls or not, but they were certainly all marvellous and always made sure they played games in which Victoria could take part. She was an absolute scream in a play they put on mimicking Mrs Thatcher and several others, using mountains of dressing-up clothes provided by Nannie.

Victoria's treatment for that week took place during their stay and would be the last before our holiday. We were hoping and praying that all would be well. Linda, Jim and the children came into the hospital to see her, which kept her from getting bored, especially when the alarm went off in one of the toilets, bringing all the nurses rushing from behind their station, only to discover it had been young Jamie, aged two, who was unable to control the urge to push the fascinating buttons.

Too soon their visit was over, and although it was sad to see them go, we had our holiday to look forward to. But I think Linda and Jim realised that in all probability they would not see Victoria again.

My parents were still in blissful ignorance of the recurrence of Victoria's illness. I could well imagine what they might be thinking about the coming holiday too, knowing that we were rather hard up at the time. It had become harder with each day that passed even to think about telling them anything. Victoria astounded me one day by asking, 'Have you told Granny and Grandad about me yet?' I replied that, no, I hadn't, as I didn't want them to fuss and I knew she wouldn't either. Then, the part that amazed me, 'Well, it's going to be a bit of a shock for them if I die.' What on earth was I to say to this? But she obviously hadn't wanted or expected an answer as she had changed the subject and was now wondering what Spain was going to be like. I couldn't help thinking she might be right. But still we didn't tell them. We would do so on our return home.

We spent a morning in the town shortly before the holiday, doing some shopping. The girls both needed new swimming costumes, shorts and tee-shirts as well as a few other bits and pieces. Why did I always seem to leave everything to the last minute? I'm afraid that is a failing of mine, but this time there was a valid reason for it, as I had never really pictured the holiday actually taking place, feeling that something would prevent our going. Now I knew that it was going to happen, although to be honest I was going away convinced that we would have to return early.

All contingencies had been taken care of. Our insurance covered a special plane home with a nurse in attendance and we had a letter with us, signed by the Consultant Radiologist, explaining exactly the nature of Victoria's illness and that should she be taken ill, she was to be repatriated immediately. We also went armed with various drugs, as well as the usual holiday first aid kit. I only hoped we would not be stopped at customs as we had no covering letter for these. We had all had a gamma-globulin injection to prevent hepatitis, as the last thing Victoria needed was to come back with an infection in her blood which would prevent her from having treatment when we returned home.

So, everything was planned down to the last detail, to ensure, as much as was possible anyway, a relaxed and trouble-free holiday. We certainly had no regrets or doubts now about going, and we never would have.

# CHAPTER
## 15

At last the great day arrived. Alan's father collected us early to take us to the airport. Our flight was due to leave at eight in the morning. It was only as we were packing that we realised that the car we had hired in Spain might well prove to be too small. When we had booked the holiday we hadn't imagined taking a wheelchair with us. Well, there was nothing we could do about it now.

The airport staff were absolutely wonderful. We were taken out to the plane by special bus, so that Victoria's chair could be put inside the plane and not in the hold with the rest of the luggage. This was so that she could use it as soon as we alighted from the plane.

The flight was nothing out of the ordinary, except that all the stewardesses seemed to be extra attentive towards Victoria. As usual, I was always terrified on take-off. This was generally calmed by a drink, but at eight o'clock in the morning I felt it was a little early to be knocking back gin and tonic, and I managed to survive the ordeal without it.

Our arrival at Malaga was marked by a sudden rush of warm air as the cabin doors were opened. Even though it had been quite warm at home before we left, it was completely different here. Within half an hour of landing, the girls and I were sitting in the airport lounge waiting for Alan. He had gone to look for the car, having already decided that he might have to make two trips to the villa in Mijas, should the car turn out to be too small for all our baggage. He soon appeared, wearing a broad grin from ear to ear, and announced that not only was there plenty of room behind the back seats but the car had a roof rack as well, so two trips would not be necessary.

It was by now nearly lunchtime and as we couldn't move into the villa until after five o'clock, we decided to drive to Fuengirola, the nearest town to Mijas, in the mountains behind, and find a nice restaurant; we were all feeling rather hungry by this time. The whole atmosphere made us feel relaxed and happy and it was hard to believe there was anything wrong.

Having whiled away a few hours with our meal and shopping for one or two items of food, we decided to make our way to the villa, although it was still well before five. We were unsure of the way and besides, there was always the chance that the previous occupants had already vacated it, leaving it ready for us.

The scenery was fabulous as we drove up the hills behind Fuengirola, the whiteness of the buildings glistening in the afternoon sun. We took one wrong turning, before finding before us what I can only describe as the villa of our dreams.

'This can't be it,' I said in disbelief. 'It's fabulous. We must have got the wrong one.'

'It's got the same name as ours, and it looks the same as the one in the photograph. I'll go up and see if the key is where it's supposed to be,' said Alan, getting out of the car.

'Ooh, it's super,' said Victoria, 'I do hope it's ours.'

'So do I,' said Joanna. 'Can we go for a swim in the pool? I'm so hot.'

'We might not be able to get in yet, even if it is ours. It did say after five o'clock in the travel agent's letter,' I reminded them. It must be the right one; I could see Alan approaching waving the keys in his hand. The girls rushed out of the car. 'Wait until you see the pool,' Alan told them.

It was indeed a lovely house, so much nicer than we had anticipated, almost a dream come true. Not just the villa itself, but the pool set in a colourful garden, full of the kind of blooms one expects in Spain—bougainvillaea, jacaranda and olive trees.

In no time at all the girls were splashing about in the pool to their hearts content. This was something that had worried both of us and Dr Martin as well: would Victoria be able to swim? Her breath was very short and we feared she would get miserable and frustrated by seeing Joanna splashing about and not being able to join in. To combat this, we had brought along a small inflatable dinghy, so that she would not feel left out, and would be able to get around in the water. This, swimming costumes apart, was one of the first items to be unpacked.

The girls spent hours in the pool, as we all did. Thank heavens we had brought the dinghy. Curiously enough, after just a few days Victoria began to venture into the water without it and was soon swimming as she had done before. After a week she was swimming under the water, having bought a pair of goggles in one of the local shops! We couldn't believe it. Had she somehow been miraculously cured? I voiced my thoughts to Alan, but we had both heard her coughing during the night and knew we were only kidding ourselves. Sometimes it was heart-rending to listen to her, knowing there was nothing either of us could do to help. We did have some medicine with us that seemed to ease it a little, but apart from this there was nothing. It was just one of the terrible features of the disease and one that would continue to get worse.

In some way I'm sure Victoria was aware that she had not much longer with us. Looking at the photos of the holiday, her facial expression always appears remarkably serene and contented, without any hint of what she was going through. It had been commented on, even before we saw the photos. I can't really put it into words as I would like to, but to me, anyway, it was as if she was privileged to know something none of us knew.

One evening when we were eating out at a local restaurant as we often did, Alan was talking, and as I gazed at the view from our table to the sea, Victoria and I just happened to look at each other. She gave me the most beautiful smile. It was as if we were the only two people there; she seemed almost to radiate happiness and comfort to me. In that second I was aware that she knew what was going to happen and that she was aware that I knew too. As if she was telling me she knew and that she wasn't frightened. I can't describe it any more vividly, nor my feelings at the time, but I remember it now as if it were yesterday.

Our fabulous holiday drifted on in seemingly endless days of sunshine and cloudless skies. By now I was fairly confident that we would not have to rush home, as I had so pessimistically believed at the beginning. We didn't do much sightseeing. Victoria found it extremely tiring and the Spaniards did tend to stare at the little girl in the wheelchair with only one leg. Her breathing problems had forced her to stop using the artificial limb some weeks before, and consequently she hadn't even brought it with her on holiday. I was told after our return that it is natural sympathy with the child that made the Spanish people stare so, not morbid curiosity, but Victoria was beginning to find it rather a strain.

We were more than content with each other's company around the pool, able to eat what and when we liked. Just pleasing ourselves was wonderful, but too soon the idyll came to an end and we were packing our suitcases for the journey home. None of us really wanted to leave the peace we had found in our own little corner of Spain. Or perhaps it was because we had some inkling of the tragic events that were to overtake us so soon?

Almost as soon as we landed Victoria started coughing. She didn't want to get off the plane.

'Can't we just stay on it and go straight back, please, Daddy?' she asked. How much we all wished we could do just that. But nothing goes on forever, however much we may wish it could.

We arrived home late on Thursday night to torrential rain, a power cut and cows wandering across our partly seeded new lawn, much to the delight of Victoria. 'It's just like being back in Spain,' she cried. Alan's parents both remarked on how well she was looking and indeed she was. This was, I was sure, not only due to all that sunshine and fresh air, but also because she had eaten much more in the last two weeks than she had over the previous two months at home. This had surprised us, but we were very pleased too. Surely it was a good sign?

Throughout the weekend Victoria's breathing deteriorated considerably, the pain increasing at the same time, and she was beginning to look unwell now. If only there was something we could do?

Alan's dad had taken to popping in nearly every day since the cancer had returned, although we tried to dissuade him. We felt sure Victoria might begin to wonder why. If she did, she certainly never mentioned it. However, he called round on the Sunday after our arrival home. Having eaten so well on holiday, Victoria had had virtually nothing since our return, apart from the odd cup of tea. Today was no exception, she was very ill. As usual she put on an extremely brave face when Grandad arrived. It must have been a terrible strain for her, and I could see the relief on her face after he had left. She was by now accepting the odd pain-killer which was a sign to us of how much pain she must be bearing. We still had to persuade her that the pain-killers were purely to make her feel more comfortable, that there was no shame in asking for them.

That night Victoria was fairly late going to bed and even after Joanna had been asleep for hours, she still wanted Alan and me to stay with her, as if she didn't want to lose sight of us. We stayed gladly, just talking and looking at books and the things she had bought in Spain. Even after she had fallen asleep she called me several times. In the early hours I managed to get her to take a pain-killer.

'I'll go and make you a cup of tea to take it with, shall I?' She nodded. She was by now very ill. My heart felt as if it were breaking as I looked at her slim body lying there. 'I'm dying Mummy,' she said, simply telling me. Oh God, where would I find the strength to bear it? I just knelt by the bed and put my arms around her. We had no need of words.

'Can Joanna come and sit with me while you make the tea?' she asked. I wondered if I would be able to rouse her, but she was already awake and willingly came to sit by her sister's side. It was with tears in my eyes that I left them together, holding hands.

Should I phone Dr Martin? She had said that we could do so at any time if we were at all worried about anything. But then we had an appointment at the hospital with her in just a couple of hours time. I talked it over with Alan, who went in to see Victoria. She insisted that we didn't phone the doctor.

We dropped Joanna off at Alan's mother's, who was going to take her to school, as we had to be at the hospital very early. Victoria seemed to be a bit brighter, but was it all forced to stop us worrying? Alan took her for the chest X-ray while I went in to see Dr Martin as I wanted to speak to her before she saw Victoria. We knew that she would hardly even admit to being ill in front of her.

The chest X-ray revealed that one lung had collapsed, causing much of her difficulty in breathing. This is something that can happen to anyone. However, it wasn't the lung that had already partly collapsed some weeks before, so she was only breathing with roughly two-thirds of one lung, yet she had made so little of it. She must have been in a great deal of pain.

We took her to the children's ward, where a specialist in thoracic surgery would, by means of a local anaesthetic, insert a small tube to 'reflate' the lung. She didn't particularly want to go through with this but at the same time realised that it would make her feel much more comfortable. Alan and I went down for a coffee afterwards, leaving her chatting and laughing with the nurses, telling them all about our holiday.

When we returned, she smiled at us as we approached the bed. She was feeling so much better, she said, and she certainly looked much more relaxed than at any time since we were back. We chatted for about half an hour. She was due to go down for a chest X-ray shortly to make sure that the lung had inflated. Just as the porter appeared with the trolley to take her down, she began to cough badly. I rushed to help her as she struggled to sit up. My heart missed a beat as she seemed to pass out. Someone thrust an oxygen mask into my shaking hands and as I heard the sound of the alarm bell ringing, I desperately held the mask over her face. I realised that I was achieving nothing as the mask was taken from me. I ran from the bedside unable to control my tears, dimly aware of the doctor and more nurses approaching. Was someone pushing a cardiac arrest trolley? I knew then what had happened, and yet as one of the staff nurses showed Alan and me into a small room normally used by the doctors, I asked, 'She will be all right, won't she?' I could see that the poor girl just didn't know what to say. It was Alan who answered, 'Yes, of course she will.' I looked at him in amazement. Surely he knew as well as I did what had happened? He held me close telling me not to worry, they would do everything they could for her. I knew then that he was as aware as I was of the immediate danger. Was he controlling himself and keeping his emotions in check for my sake? It is strange looking back that one of us was always in control enough to comfort the other; we seldom broke down together. And on the rare occasions when we did, one of us was always in enough control to help the other. It was almost uncanny, but perhaps it is just the natural defence mechanism of the mind enabling us each to cope with such traumas. It was certainly not something that occurred consciously or with any control on either part.

We sat silently, our hands clasped, wondering what was going on in the ward. The staff nurse left to make some tea. About five or ten minutes passed before the door opened again and the doctor entered. We both looked up expectantly, but one glance at his face was enough to confirm what we already feared.

'I'm sorry,' he said, 'but I'm afraid she . . . she's died. We did everything we could but it was no use. I'm so sorry . . .'

Alan and I just collapsed into each other's arms, oblivious to everything but our grief. Never before had we felt as we did then. Completely and utterly devastated is hardly an adequate way to describe our feelings. Despite knowing that her life would inevitably be cut short by the return of the cancer, I suppose we went on hoping and praying that it would not be so. There was nothing that could cushion the blow, no words just then to comfort us. One might think that having had four months to come to terms with it we should have been more prepared for the end? I don't think that is possible if one is still to have hope. The very fact that the date was June 27, just four days after our return from what we now think of as a God-given holiday, when she had seemed so well and happy, only served to heighten our misery. Yet it is said that death, the one thing we can be certain will happen to all of us at some time, always comes at a time when it is least expected. For although I may have had a vague feeling about it, I certainly didn't expect it at that moment.

The doctor came and sat with us. It was only as he started to speak that I realised, with a shock, how upset he was. 'I'm so sorry,' he said quietly, 'I just don't know what to say, she was such a lovely little child . . .' He couldn't go on. I reached out to touch his arm, to try and comfort him. 'Please, you mustn't feel badly about it, we both know you did all you could for her.' What could I say? I felt so sorry for him, he was younger than Alan and me, in his late twenties. He had always shown us kindness and great compassion and Victoria had thought he was super. We sat in silence for some while, each with our own thoughts. It was the doctor who broke the silence, 'I know it's hard, but you must try and take comfort from the fact that if it hadn't happened this way, she would certainly have suffered a great deal more than she did. When I saw the X-rays this morning when you came in, I couldn't believe it.'

'Were they bad then?' I asked. 'Yes,' he answered, 'I was just hoping you wouldn't ask to see them.' He stayed with us for some time, longer than he could spare, I'm sure. The way he spoke to us made us forget that he was doing his job and was still on duty. I only wish that all bereaved parents were treated with the same degree of sympathy. We were sorry to see him go but we had to start to learn to cope on our own.

# CHAPTER
## 16
---

Victoria had been able to enjoy life to the full right to the end, and had never had to spend her days bedridden or in hospital, apart from during the chemotherapy treatment. She, more than anyone, would have hated things to have been otherwise. At least, as the doctor said, she had been spared further and much worse suffering. And had probably been more energetic in the last ten months of her life than many of us are in a lifetime, always with a joie de vivre that was utterly infectious, dismissing any pain or discomfort that she must have felt as little more than a nuisance.

It was these reminiscences that we had to cling to now, if we were not to sink into the depths of despair, however hard it proved to try and remember them. We hadn't yet come to terms with the fact that she was no longer with us. It seemed so unreal, just thinking over and over that never again would we hold her in our arms and tell her we loved her. Never again would we hear the sound of her voice. Thank God I had kept all her drawings (as I had Joanna's too), to remind me of her creativity. We just couldn't begin to imagine life at home without her.

Alan was by now almost inconsolable. I felt I had no tears left, just an emptiness inside. He took himself to task so much. 'Why did we let her have that tube put in?' he sobbed. 'She kept saying she didn't want to come in and I just kept telling her that it would make her feel better. If I hadn't she might still be here.'

'Oh, my darling, you mustn't ever think that. It *did* make her feel better, you could see that she looked much more comfortable. It could have happened any time. It would have been much worse if she'd collapsed at home.' We were trying to convince each other, trying to come to terms with it all and to face up to life without her. As Alan said, we mustn't forget we still had Joanna, we had to remember her, and as everyone kept reminding us in the next few days, life goes on. I did become a little sick of hearing that clichéd phrase, but we both knew that it was true.

We stayed on at the hospital for some time, unable to return immediately to the outside world where we had to face Joanna and our respective families with such heart-breaking news. I became more and more anxious on behalf of my own parents, knowing that they had been unaware of just how ill Victoria had been over the last four months: indeed, they hadn't been told that the cancer had returned. I now seriously began to question the wisdom of having hidden it from them, despite taking advice. However, it was too late for recriminations now; I would just have to face them as best I could and hope they would realise and accept the reasons behind our decision. Naturally Alan was worried on behalf of his parents, especially as only a short time ago he had telephoned his mother to say that Victoria was so much better and that he would be over to collect Joanna later while I stayed the night at the hospital.

It was Joanna, naturally, whose reaction concerned us the most. How was it going to affect her? Not only had she lost a sister but she had lost her best friend. Just how does one tell a little girl of only eight years old that she would never see her sister again?

Momentarily, these tortuous thoughts were brushed aside as the door opened and in walked Neil and Jill. We were both so grateful for their presence. What kind fate had decreed that they should be in the hospital at that precise moment? I wondered briefly if one of the other nurses had phoned them, knowing how much support they had both given us since Jill had become Victoria's favourite nurse on her first admission to hospital. It seemed so long ago now, but in fact it had only been ten months. They explained that Neil had come to the hospital to visit one of his parishioners and Jill had come along to see all her old friends in the children's ward. Of course they had not expected to see us there nor to discover the tragic news, but I shall always be grateful for their company at that time.

Eventually, we decided it was time to leave for home: after all, we were only postponing what we knew we had to face. It was not easy to say goodbye to all the staff, and we didn't attempt to, knowing they respected how we felt. Without exception they had been wonderful, doing all they could to ease our pain and comfort us, when we knew they felt much as we did. We would always remember the way in which they treated Victoria and for the many kindnesses they had shown to us. Wistfully I looked back to a time in April, the thirteenth, to be exact. It was Joanna's birthday and Victoria, who had been in hospital for her regular treatment, had informed the staff. When Joanna arrived to see her sister, she was thrilled not only to receive a lovely present, but a super cake as well, complete with eight candles.

All this seemed so long ago, almost as if I had imagined it. It must also seem a trivial thing to have been on my mind just then, but maybe it was thinking of these little things that kept us going through the next few terrible days. I cannot pretend we sailed through it all with ease: it was the most difficult time that any of us had had to face. To lose any close relative is always distressing, but to lose a child is something else entirely; it seemed as though the pain and heartache we felt would never diminish. All our thoughts centred on whom we had lost. We could not even begin to think how we were going to cope without her.

Slowly and in silence we made our way to the car. 'Shall I drive?' I asked Alan, who still looked dreadful. I just felt numb by now. I didn't want to feel anything. 'No, it's all right, I will,' he answered. We had decided that before going to his parents' house, we would go home first. We were just putting things off again, but we felt we had to collect our thoughts away from the hospital, and anyway we didn't want to arrive before Dad was home from work. Few words were spoken once we reached home. We had no need of them, what was there to say? I had a stiff drink, which really did nothing to alleviate the way I felt. 'We'd better go now,' I said after a while. 'It will only be much worse if we keep putting it off.' 'I suppose you're right,' Alan said, 'but I'm dreading it all the same.'

We were somehow able to find the strength necessary to face our ordeal. I think we both felt eased once we had shared our feelings with our friends and family, although

I often felt we were only moving the burden onto other shoulders. Much of the weight was lifted, for me anyway, by the fact that my parents took it all so well, never once questioning our motives. The reactions of our immediate families were predictable and it would take everyone a long time to accept what had happened. Joanna took it very hard, but even so she would always try and comfort us, putting her arms around us and saying, 'Don't cry, Victoria has gone to Heaven,' and I'm sure that she is right. I have to cling onto the hope that one day I will see her again.

It is said that the pain of grieving lessens with the passage of time, but I feel that it is more a question of learning to live with it, learning to remember the many happy times. But I will never get over it. Nor will we ever forget her. We don't want to. She was part of our family and always will be. Although I spent a lot of time at the beginning asking, why, why did it have to happen to our daughter, the experience has only served to strengthen my faith. I can well understand that it might have the very opposite effect on others, but I have gained a lot of strength from believing as I do. I was confirmed at Easter, the year after her death. I had been to confirmation classes in my early teens, but at that time had rebelled against it all as irrelevant. Although I had been brought up to go to Sunday School, my parents never really went to church except at Christmas, Easter and the usual weddings etc. And now, some two years after being confirmed, I am still not a regular church go-er. I believe in God, but I cannot see the need to declare it in public every Sunday. Perhaps I'm wrong, I haven't got the right attitude, but I would nevertheless consider myself a Christian, one with all the usual human failings, failings that perhaps those who openly profess their somewhat self-righteous faith seldom admit to. Victoria had gained strength from her simple faith, and who was I to doubt it?

We don't visit Victoria's grave regularly. She isn't there. She's still with us in so many ways. About three days after her death I realised that our holiday photos would be ready. Should I go and collect them? We hesitated for some time. 'I think I will,' I said, 'we don't have to look at them if we don't want to.' But I knew of course that once we had collected them they would prove irresistible. In the end we were so pleased to have them. They gave us great comfort. To see how well and happy Victoria had looked, only ten days or so before, was truly wonderful.

We have learned, albeit slowly, to adjust to life without her, to accept that we are now three instead of four, that when a door opens, it will not be Victoria who walks through it. I can't pretend that it has been easy and it is a gradual process. It does not happen overnight or even in weeks. I still find it hard, nearly two years later, to accept that she has gone. I consider myself very lucky in having a close relationship with Alan. We are always able to talk about things and are closer now than ever. How can something like that drive couples apart? Yet in some cases it does. We are both lucky too in having Joanna, who has been, and still is, a great comfort to us.

One thing that has been brought home to me, is that people don't like to talk about death. Is it fear of the unknown? Well, whatever it is, one of the most difficult things we had to cope with were other people's reactions. I don't mean family or even close friends, but acquaintances. Looking back, I can appreciate how they felt, that they didn't know what to say. Had I not been through it, I would probably be the same. But there were times when I wanted to scream at people, 'My daughter is dead. Don't you care?' There were even some who crossed the road rather than speak to me, which I found very hard to take. But, would I have behaved any differently if the circumstances had been reversed? I can't answer that honestly, except to say that I hope I would.

Life does go on and indeed it must. We have much to be thankful for, not least Joanna and of course we will always have our memories of Victoria. No-one can take those away. Indeed without her example we would certainly have found it all much harder to bear. Although I am certain that all children inflicted by life-threatening disease gain a quality that puts the rest of us to shame, I do feel that Victoria had something extra. You may say that I feel as I do because she was my daughter and naturally my thoughts and memories are coloured by that. But there are also the words of the doctors and nurses who treated her and who dealt with the same ailments in others. In particular I recall the words of Mr Steel who performed the amputation. He said, 'In my long and unhappy experience of this most unhappy disease, I have always been surprised by the resilience and courage of most children, but Victoria was quite exceptional. She will certainly never be forgotten by any of us who were lucky enough to know her.'

Our lives have been considerably enriched by the example of courage and faith shown to us by our ten-year-old daughter and I hope that others will continue to draw inspiration from her memory. I can only hope that these words might bring comfort to others and that although the end was inevitably sad, Victoria's joy of life has shone through. I found the following words in a booklet of prayers that was sent to us, and they have come to mean a great deal:

'I don't look back on it all as a matter of sorrow, I thank God that such a lovely thing was ours for so long.'

Victoria has left us with much to be grateful for, not least the great courage she showed which was such an inspiration to all who knew her. She left us too with a legacy of hope for the future, and the fund set up after her death, bearing her name, serves as a reminder.

# Postscript I

The Victoria Hart Cancer Research Trust was instigated just a few days after Victoria's death, the idea being that people might wish to donate to cancer research rather than send flowers. We were astounded by the response. Hundreds of pounds came pouring in after it was reported in the *Daily Mail*, and in the first two weeks alone nearly £13,000 was raised, mostly from people who only knew of Victoria through the media. Many of the donations were anonymously sent and a large number were from old age pensioners who could ill afford such a gift. A trust was soon established and charitable status was granted in 1984. The aims of the fund are twofold. Firstly it serves to aid the Royal Marsden hospital with its various fundraising activities. Victoria herself had been shocked on her visit there that the hospital was appealing for funds to buy a cancer scanner, and she wanted to undertake a sponsored swim to help them. Secondly it proposes to aid all forms of cancer research, but in particular those projects concerned with children. So the fund continues and we hope it will do so for many years to come, in the hope that one day in the future cancer may become a thing of the past.

The address of the Victoria Hart Cancer Research Trust is:
The Midland Bank plc, 105 Mount Pleasant,
Tunbridge Wells, Kent TN1 1QP.
A proportion of the royalties from this book
will be donated to the Trust.

# Postscript II

Many people will be interested to know how Demelza Spruce has fared. She had her leg amputated because of the same Osteogenic Sarcoma as Victoria's, and I am delighted to say that now, nearly three years later, she is thriving. She suffered a slight setback in the summer of 1984 when two small tumours were discovered, one on each of her lungs. These were successfully removed, with Demelza herself showing enormous courage and fortitude throughout her ordeal. She is now happily settled at school where she takes part in all their activities. She has also learnt to play the piano and goes swimming once a week, which she only learnt to do after the amputation. She is also a member of her local Brownie pack and has even taken a course in trampolining. She is a well-adjusted and happy child, who has never lost her sense of fun, something I think that all these children can teach the rest of us, who tend sometimes to let even the smallest of problems become major issues in our lives. Of course she still has to go for her regular checkups at the hospital, but we shall always hope and pray that she will continue to lead a full and happy life.